SUNDAY ADELAJA

RAISING THE NEXT GENERATION OF STEVE JOBS AND BILL GATES

... HOW TO CONVERT YOUR INNER ENERGY INTO TANGIBLE PRODUCTS

Sunday Adelaja
RAISING THE NEXT GENERATION
OF STEVE JOBS AND BILL GATES

©2017 Sunday Adelaja

ISBN 978-1-908040-67-1

Cover design by Oleksander Bondaruk
Interior design by Oleksander Bondaruk

CONTENTS

INTRODUCTION

*One idea (energy) lights a thousand
candles.*
RALPH WALDO EMERSON

Everything is energy and everything starts with energy, however vague or small. Everything started with one form of energy. Every voyage ever made, every journey ever travelled, every invention, every dress, every dish is a product of a man's single thought that was transformed into a form of energy. All movies, all skills, all experiences, all goods, all services and products, all knowledge, all commerce, all industry, all medicine, all governments, all nations, all competitions and leagues began as a product of one man's idea, inspiration and energy. An energy is the very foundation upon which the world is built and the raw material with which everything in it is made. Energies, which some call ideas are powerful.

The truly poor man in the world today is the man without an idea. Poorer than the man without an idea is the man who is not seeking to have an idea. The poorest man of all however, is the man who though has an idea is not able to convert his inspiration, idea and energy into a product.

Such a man has missed a golden opportunity in life to change his world and contribute meaningfully to it. He has missed the chance to touch his world and edge his name in gold. He has missed a chance to truly live. If you are not able to express your own original energy and ideas, if you do not listen to your own being, you would have betrayed yourself. It means, the world was never able to meet you personally. It means the world was never able to understand what you carried or why you were on earth in the first place.

Having an idea and not birthing it is akin to being barren. Imagine the difficulty and challenge of being married for months and years and not being able to bring forth fruits. Imagine the pain and the disappointment that comes with it. More measure of sorrow and despair accompanies an inspiration, thought, idea and all forms of such energy which was not brought forth to the world. The full weight of a man is not in just his ideas, but in what he is able to do with it.

Do you know Charles Babbage? The man considered to be the 'father of computer'. He designed several models of the modern day computer but never built any working model successfully. He had the energy but failed in building the product. He was never able to birth his ideas. His theories were later used to build working models which meant those designs could have worked at the time. He lost a golden opportunity and the world did too. Imagine what the world would have been today if Charles built those computers during 1812 to 1819, up to two hundred years ago when he had the inspiration and the idea. What would the world have been if the idea of the computer was born two hundred years earlier? Failure to discover, work on and convert your energy and ideas into products will not only affect you, but leave a lasting damage on your world.

The big problem many people today have is not the problem of having inspiration. Inspiration and ideas are not magical, most people have ideas. The trouble however is the inability to birth the ideas that have been conceived. A lot of people have simply given up on their ideas, laying it down in the grave of their minds. This explains to you that there are two kinds of graves; the first is the physical where we lay everything that ceases to live and exist. The second is in the mind where all thoughts, ideas, revelations, insights, rhema, experiences and concepts which we failed to give life to die and are permanently buried.

This is only similar to the case of abortion. Abortion equals termination which is putting an end to the beginning of a process, putting an end to the beginning of a life. Whenever we put an end to the thoughts, energy, ideas and inspiration that God has given us, we are guilty of same effects and consequences of abortion. No one else can abort your idea. Only you can put your idea to death.

Some people in life have wondered why they are so ineffective and why it is only a few people who seem to be all alone on top of the ladder of creativity. Such people view the likes of Steve Jobs, Bill Gates, Warren Buffet, and Mark Zuckerberg as geniuses. Some concluded that such men are just plain lucky or some god somewhere has favored them.

They fail to see that there are principles that these men apply which have made them who they are. One area where these men differ from majority in the world today is in their ability to convert and bring their ideas to life.

Well, maybe not everyone who failed to birth their idea did not try. Many people try and give up. When such people have tried and not succeeded, perhaps at the first attempt, they rationalize, conclude, give it up or say perhaps 'it is not God's time or 'it is not God's will'. The lack of the appropriate knowledge to use in giving life to their idea has made them give up too soon. Such people give up on life, give up on hope and give up on themselves. Little wonder, depression is on an everyday increase.

This book will bring you into a whole new realm of understanding. You will begin to see that anyone can be a genius too. You will appreciate that everyone has an idea and can indeed work on such ideas. You will learn how to convert your ideas into products. You will learn the principles of life that guide the creation of products. Together, we will also explore the lives of some select men. We will learn their secrets and why they are problem solvers. At the end of the book, you will gain the ability and know all it takes to be among the emerging set of Steve Jobs and Bill Gates.

This book is all about conversion, you will understand why conversion is very important to your ideas. In fact, without conversion, Ideas are useless. It is conversion that brings life into your ideas, that birth meaning into it. For example the idea of this book was first a thought in my mind, it had to undergo the process and steps of conversion for it to become this book you are holding right now in your hand. If I chose to do nothing about it, it wouldn't have come forth. Now think about how many ideas had died in your mind just because you did nothing about them. An idea is only an idea until you breathe life into it. You breathe life into your idea by converting it into real products. Every good idea, inspiration and energy that comes must be trapped and brought forth into the form that the world can benefit from. That is a secret of greatness and effectiveness.

My passion for writing this book is to ensure that henceforth, no one especially you, dear reader goes to the grave with all the ideas and potential that you have been given by God. I want to show you practically how you can begin to bring products out of your gifts, thoughts and revelation. I want to show you that your idea too can transform the world like the iPad and Microsoft have done. In fact, creating such products will no longer be a big dream for you. I want to show you that you too can be among the next league of winners. I want you to escape the group of those who though came, never saw and never conquered. There were a lot who lived but said nothing, did nothing and were nothing. One of the favorite quotes from my late good friend, Myles Munroe goes thus:

"The wealthiest place in the world is not the gold mines of South America or the oil fields of Iraq or Iran. They are not the diamond mines of South Africa or the banks of the world. The wealthiest place on the planet is just down the road. It is the cemetery. There lie buried companies that were never started, inventions that were never made, best-selling books that were never written, and masterpieces that were never painted. In the cemetery is buried the greatest treasure of untapped potential."

You cannot die with your ideas and potential. Everything in you must be entirely maximized and used up. You cannot afford to fail. Remember that the whole creation is waiting for you. It's your time to win.

FOR THE LOVE OF GOD, CHURCH AND NATION
SUNDAY ADELAJA.

PREFACE

The year was 1976, the city was Los Altos, California and the place was a garage. Two young men (one of whom was 21-year old and the other 26-year old) seemed busy working on something. One of them had just finished a summer job at HP factory, but the two share a mutual love for electronics. So within the garage, both of these young men were working on some electronics and electronic spare parts.

Nothing seemed spectacular about their work as different pieces of electronic parts lied around the garage. Nothing seemed strange either as both boys appeared as just two young people playing with objects. The only thing that was strange in the garage was in these two boys' heads, the two young men claim to have an idea, an inspiration that will change the world. This belief they had seemed to also reflect in the tireless manner and their attitude to their work.

What idea were the two young men working on? They have got an idea that will help place the modern computers into people's pockets or that will make the computer so much smaller. The average computer at this time was so big that a truck was needed to make its delivery to any location, a computer that big often came with a very small memory. Sometimes, just one computer filled an entire building for a memory of just about 5 Megabytes. By the way most laptop computers today have memories of about 200 times the size of those old computers.

However, these two young men believed that they could work on that problem. They believed they could develop a brand of computer, faster computers with larger memories that could fit into anyone's pocket or at least sit on your table. That was totally inconceivable at the time, in fact how could two young boys think they could do it? It was a crazy idea, but one which if successful would change the world.

Hard they worked, doing everything to birth their idea and convert their inspiration into product. Eventually, on 28th Aug 1976, Steve Jobs and Steve Wozniak showed off the Apple I at the Personal Computing Festival in Atlantic City. It was a milestone in the history of modern computers and one of several milestones to follow. The world would never remain the same.

Steve Jobs alongside his friend, another Steve had succeeded in changing the face of the computer for the modern world. The world will never recover from the impact of these young men especially Steve Jobs who later went ahead to design some more historic feats in the world of computers.

For example, on 23rd June 2003, Steve Jobs unveiled the Power Mac G5, the world's fastest computer, at the time. This is aside the many other land mark products that he blessed the world with, some of which includes the Apple II (Launched in June 1977, the Apple II was the first successful mass-marketed personal computer in the world) Lisa

Computers, the Macintosh, the iPod, the MacBook Pro, the iPhone, the MacBook Air, the iPad. Each of these products brought about revolution to the world, especially to the world of technology and business.

A year before Steve Jobs and Steve Wozniak developed the Apple I, another young man and his friend had made another amazing discovery about computer operating systems, the language with which computers interact with man and by which we understand them. This invention was extra-ordinary and it changed the face of the earth. It simply meant by this invention now, anyone can perform most tasks on the personal computer just with a few simple commands. This was another major milestone in the history of computer in the world. The young man was called Bill Gates and his friend was called Paul Allen.

Bill Gates would later leave his prestigious school (Harvard University) where he had been enrolled to study law in order to pursue his core passion of programming and creating operating systems for the computer. Each of the operating systems he produced changed the face of technology in the world in a significant way. All of these achievements have made him the richest man in the world till date and one that has been so over many years.

While this book is not about computers, it is definitely about men, young men who were able to bring their ideas to life. It is about the principles that these men, Bill Gates and Steve Jobs who are ordinary like every one of us came up with ideas, and birthed the ideas that changed the world.

Because principles are timeless, it's same principle that has been employed by every inventor in history, from Benjamin Franklin to Nikolas Tesla, to Thomas Edison etc. It is the principles of conversion. These are same principles you must employ if you must convert your energy, idea and inspiration from being just mere ideas into being products that will change the face of the earth and the way certain things are done in the world.

This book is to inspire every one of us to do same, to convert whatever ideas that we have into products that will change the world.

If you can have energy, idea and inspiration, you can have a product and invention. If you can have a product and invention, you can also leave your steps in the sand of time.

Let us now get into the book and discover timeless principles that will make you emerge in the league of the next generation of Steve Jobs and Bill Gates.

CHAPTER 1

HOW TO CONVERT INVISIBLE ENERGY TO TANGIBLE PRODUCT

Let him who would move the world first move himself.
SOCRATES

Everything is energy. Physicists have defined energy as the ability to do work. By this definition, you realize that everything is energy. The things that have been created and the things that do not yet exist are all energy. The things especially that we call anointing is energy as well. When we fail to understand this, we complicate our life, our existence and our spirituality.

Our spirituality is actually energy as well. Your life is energy, everything is energy. Walls are energy, prayers are energy, phones are energy, computers are energy, everything is energy. When therefore we talk about spiritual energy, we are talking about God's energy. His word and His spirit are some of the greatest energy that is available on earth.

Energy is everywhere and everything is energy.

HOW DO YOU CONVERT YOUR INVISIBLE ENERGY INTO TANGIBLE PRODUCTS?

How do you benefit from all your spiritual exercises, how do you convert your spiritual experiences into products?

How do we convert our thoughts into tangible products? How do we convert our prayers into tangible products? How do we convert our relationship with God into tangible products? How do we convert our spiritual experiences into tangible products? How do we convert rhema into tangible and physical products? How do we convert ideas and words into physical manifestations? How do we convert values like faith, love, passion, kindness etc into tangible manifestation?

All the spiritual things that we talk about like the Bible, the word of God, prayers, and virtues like kindness, faith and love can be converted into material products. All of them must and should be converted to benefit the earth.

Christians often are only fond of talking and preaching about these things without physically birthing them. When we only talk about them without birthing them physically for people to see and experience, we leave the world confused.

The first thing that must be done for invisible energy to become tangible product is that we need inspiration.

For example, when you pray and you are in relationship with God, you are in a different realm. In that realm, your physical body in which you exist cannot soar. The only way that your physical body could access and be blessed and be inspired by the things happening in the spirit is through the waves of the spirit. Some people call it vibration of the spirit, we will rather call it inspiration. When you are truly in the presence of God, what that gives you first of all is a 'goosebumps' experience.

These goosebumps allow you know that you are in the frequency of the spirit and that you are in the Holy Ghost and that you are near God. It helps you know you are in the right frequency and the right wave. That movement, experience and incubation of the spirit is stimulating your spirit man or otherwise called inner man. That interaction of the spirit of God and your own spirit is called inspiration. When the spirit of God moves upon you, it begins to inspire you and your body responds as goose bumps. It is this experience that births the heat and that unusual sensation. It also shows that you are now open for the spirit's move.

A lot of people go to church just for that experience. Many jump, scream, dance, shout, fall in response to the frequency and the waves of the spirit.

HOW TO RESPOND TO INSPIRATION

The best way to respond to inspiration is to convert your inspiration. The best way to respond however to those goose bumps experiences is to respond through conversion. The best way to respond is to learn to convert that inspiration and frequency into products.

The way this happens is that when you begin to feel that inspiration and presence, you must know that the spirit of God is near you and that God is close to you. You must know that God is everywhere and has infinite knowledge, God is the depth of wisdom and the source of all understanding, he has all the answers and everything is in him. Now once you begin to feel that nearness to God, the next thing is to begin to submit yourself to God at that particular time and open up your mind.

In Genesis 1, God observed the void and emptiness and devastation. The next thing that God did was to release his spirit, his frequency, his waves, his energy, his dimension and presence over that emptiness and void. We must also act in the same way, when we come to God as empty, void, shapeless and in our devastation. In his presence his spirit begins to interact with our spirit to deal with every darkness and emptiness of life. With this dealing, though our bodies cannot respond appropriately just by falling, our minds must begin to respond appropriately by functioning at that time.

Unfortunately when many pray, they switch off their mind. When you go to pray, that is the time to open up your mind and connect your mind to that frequency. That wave and anointing and presence must open you up in the spirit and you must begin to ask God questions and let him speak to you. That presence and anointing and quickness of the spirit must not be wasted, it must be converted immediately on the level of the mind.

When you sing in worship and you are in praise, you must immediately begin to convert your experience into IDEAS.

Release your mind to begin to think and let your mind begin to search for answers. You must begin to ask God questions and to begin to seek to resolve a particular problem. You must begin to think deeply now about your research. You must begin to brood over your pertinent questions just like a chicken broods over her eggs. You must begin to think the same way. This is what births results.

If you are looking for answers to resolve a particular problem, within that brooding and that thinking process lies the answer. Your spirit which is already being stimulated can catch what God is saying at that particular time. This is what must happen daily when you pray.

HOW TO RECEIVE IDEAS FROM GOD

God does not speak like a radio or cassette player, God does everything like a seed and in a seed form.

So in spite of how much the spirit of God comes to you, he will first drop into your spirit man a seed or a word. He will drop into your mind a thought or idea. This is what I refer to as seed.

That seed, thought, word or inspiration will lead you and give you an idea. Embracing that idea with a mind that is already developed brings solutions. Brooding on that one word or idea multiplies into several and the opening up of several words. This is your mind working actually in tune and in synchrony with the Spirit of God. That one thought is capable to become anything; a machine, an invention, a book, a company, a corporation etc.

However the level to which your mind is already developed determines the depth and extent of that thought and of answers that it can bring about.

With the invisible energy, you feel impressed. You feel the invisible energy in prayer, in praise and worship, when you read the bible, when you feel the frequency of God's presence.

Again I must reiterate that this experience requires the opening up of your mind.

Many people always think that they need to charge their spirit or make their spirit find God. This is not correct. No one knows the spirit of God like the spirit that is already in Man. Your spirit is already one with the spirit of God. The challenge is bringing your spirit to understand what the spirit of God is trying to communicate to you. Now, you see that the problem is with your mind, not your spirit. When the spirit is already brooding over your spirit like I explained, then your mind needs to become active.

In spite of any brooding and even if you are immersed in the Holy Ghost physically, if your mind is empty, nothing results. Your mind will still not understand because it is not prepared, It becomes a mere waste of experience and spiritual exercises in futility. Your mind must always be prepared and connected or glued to download from the realm of the spirit. This is totally crucial.

Many people have a habit of suspending their mind claiming they are in the presence of God, nothing can be more wasteful. It is like a student in a school environment who does not want to make use of his mind.

1 Corinthians 2:10 explains that *"God has revealed all things (them) to us through His Spirit. For the Spirit searches all things, yes, the deep things of God."*

God's spirit and our spirit are always working together. Your spirit is always searching the spirit of God and vice versa.

Verses eleven and twelve state:

"For what man knows the things of a man except the spirit of the man which is in him? Even so no one knows the things of God except the Spirit of God. Now we have received, not the spirit of the world, but the Spirit who is from God, that we might know the things that have been freely given to us by God."

From this scriptures, God's spirit and ours are always interacting. Our mind poses the challenge often when it lacks understanding, thus it reduces anointing into mere goosebumps because our mind does not know what to do with the experiences. The mind of many people lack the understanding of what the spirit of God is trying to communicate.

THE MOST IMPORTANT PART
OF YOU IS YOUR MIND

In order to know the communication of the spirit, you must understand first with your mind and not degrade the supernatural experiences into mere feelings.

Hence, our spirit must find its connection to our mind. This first step is totally absolute. We convert the energy into inspiration, Inspiration must then be converted into thoughts and ideas.

Without learning to convert inspiration, you can only share experiences of feelings, emotions and not thoughts. You can feel goosebumps but lack ideas. Knowledgeable people know how to convert their inspiration into ideas. In order not to waste the inspiration of the spirit of God, please activate your mind and put it into use.

Through prayers and preaching, we gather inspiration that must become ideas. A lot of people only make noise through spiritual exercises, rather than open their notes and begin to ask questions: how can I convert this into tangible physical products? What can I do with it? What Ideas can it become? What problems can it solve?

You must learn to open your mind, don't be a shallow person. Shallow people make lots of noise during preaching without grasping anything tangible. Open your mind everywhere, inspirations can come in the kitchen, bathroom, in the gym, on the playground etc.

The end point of inspiration must not just be mere words, but also thoughts and ideas. With a powerful taught mind, a little idea is embraced. A little idea when sown and when it germinates grows into big understandings, insights, revelations etc with which any problem on earth can become tackled.

This is the concept of prophecy. When real prophets prophesy, normally words are dropped into the human spirit. Once the word is released, then others flow and these words are embraced by faith. Speaking and embracing these words cause other words to follow. This same secret makes us speak in tongues and to utter mysteries. These words and sounds released in faith cause other words and ideas to be formed and released in our spirit. God does not give all the words and prophecies at same time. He releases them in bit and with faith more is drawn out from the spirit.

Through understanding these words, prophecies etc can be converted into other things.

People who write songs also share in this secret. They begin with a word and by understanding pull out the rest from within themselves.

Now you understand what you are supposed to do with your spiritual energy and experiences. You must understand they are inspirations and must be properly converted. They are all inspirations, which can be converted when the mind is open.

PUT WHAT YOU READ INTO PROCESS

When you read anything especially a story in the bible, begin to ask and process how you can begin to convert the story into real life situations. Use your mind to process what you are reading, when you do this you hit a goldmine. When you use your mind in such a way, an idea is born, an inspiration hits you and a problem is solved.

Same things must be done when you pray and meditate. You might need to read more and do some research. You might need to find out all you can on that word that you are given. You might not have the full picture immediately, but with further studying, the picture begins to form bit by bit until you get the whole picture.

The word of the Lord is always specific. Every word is important. Every word of God is an energy and must be converted into inspiration and ideas.

WITHOUT UNDERSTANDING, THERE WILL BE NO CONVERSION

After you have converted inspiration into ideas, the second stage of converting invisible energy into physical products is what is called the stage of understanding. This also takes place in the mind. This is why the mind is the most important part of a man.

Man is made of spirit, soul and body. Though man is spirit, the most important operational element of man on the earth is his mind. The mind must be developed, everything depends on how well you have developed your mind. Your mind is primary and must be cultivated for God.

A lot of women in the world today pay so much attention to their body and physical appearance than they do to their mind. They spend countless hours in the salon yet they do so little in focusing and deliberately raising the bars of their mind. If you are to function properly, then you need your mind more on the earth than you need your spirit. This is not religious but it is the truth. This is why people who do not understand God can still excel on the earth because they have taken enough time to develop their mind. I think the development of the mind is the area where a greater percentage of Christians are deficient in the world today.

That's why the book of Proverbs pays so much attention to the mind. As the smartest man that ever lived on earth, Solomon knew this. He understood the secret, he understood his own secret, the secret is in the mind.

Understanding is implementing the word to become flesh, making ideas to become tangible. When you receive the inspiration from God, you must understand the given word. If you receive a word from God and you don't understand it, how will you be able to implement it? You need your mind to be able to paint a picture of what you have received in the spirit.

If it is in a field where your mind is already developed, this process comes to you so easy. It is people with a developed mind who can really catch and understand what God is always communicating. God is always releasing ideas. Each day comes as a parcel from God. God is raining down inventions, prospects, ideas even right now as you are reading this book. The people who discover and understand what is being rained down are not the people who pray the most but the people who have spent more time learning the subject. They are the people who have spent more time in libraries and laboratories.

YOU CAN ONLY UNDERSTAND GOD WITH A DEVELOPED MIND

A lot of people claim to hear God, but only few understand him. This is because it is impossible to clearly understand what God is saying and interpret what he is showing you unless you have a developed mind.

I am sure you have heard of the Nobel Prize, a special prize and award given to individuals in recognition of outstanding advances in science, academics and culture.

Sometimes two prize winners are in different parts of the world, yet they are working on same idea and revelation. This is because there are things released in the spirit into their own spirit. People who catch and receive these ideas do not necessarily have to be Christians. The person who receives is someone who has been working on the idea and is ready. The mind is important to God and a prepared mind is what He can work with. It doesn't matter the amount of anointing and a spiritual revelation that a man has. If the mind is not developed to understand, it will not benefit you. A dull mind cannot translate the revelation the Holy Spirit wants to bring upon the earth. Such a mind is not positioned to bring into reality the ideas of heaven.

Let me give you an example I love to illustrate, Let's say God wants to invent a super plane that can fly from Europe to America in 30 minutes and wants to put the idea in a man's mind. Who do you think will get the idea of the super jet? Is it the guy on the mountain praying everyday who does not go to school and laboratories and has no clue what a super jet is? Is he the one that will receive this? Even if God comes and reveals to him this picture, he will still not be able to fathom it. His mind cannot interpret it. Whatever pictures God is showing him will be absurdity unto him.

Even if you are the holiest of holiest persons, you will be useless on the earth if your mind has not been developed.

On the other hand, let's say we have a Japanese researcher who has spent forty years developing planes, it will be too easy for him to catch and receive. God is not a respecter of persons. God will not just land his precious ideas into your laps because you are a believer, He gives you ideas because you are ready.

God releases ideas in the spirit when you have same frequency and same wavelength with him. When the mind is sharp and prepared and adequate preparation has gone into working the mind. With God, there is nothing instant, everything takes preparation.

If thirty years is required to understand a subject, you cannot beat that. You have to pay the price of acquiring knowledge.

CAN YOU PAY THE PRICE TO WALK WITH GOD?

As a Christian, you can get inspiration every day, from the Bible, from prayers and solitude. We get all the inspiration but often cannot understand a thing or how to convert a thing. Yet, everything that God intends are all written there in the Bible. The mind of God for the earth and his people are in the scriptures. Only those with a developed mind can see it and birth it on the earth.

Unbelievers on the other hand pay a lot of price in acquiring skills and knowledge and eventually stumble on what God has been communicating to an unprepared Christian for years.

A Christian will need same level of preparation, same level of skill, same amount of knowledge to birth ideas.

Do you now understand why I did not invent the iPad even though I have spent the last thirty years of my life in God's presence? You know why you did not invent the aircraft now? Of course, we both did not study and understand the subject. You know now why Steve Jobs is not the choir member of your church or a prayer warrior. Because when you sit down all day in church and not in the libraries or laboratories, then you will not be able to invent anything. The precious time wasted in pews can be spent in the right places.

To invent iPad, it is not how much you pray that matters, rather it is how much your mind is prepared.

Bill Gates is not a pastor yet he developed Microsoft.

They have been able to conceive and internalize an idea, this gives them the capacity and ability to birth forth those ideas.

This I see is the major reason many Christians have lost efficiency. The reason many Christians are not proficient. Like I said, in order to be able to walk with God and work in his business, you need to be on his wavelength. This can only happen if you apply yourself to develop your mind into the same wavelength as his mind. This is what it means to have the mind of God.

Mark Zuckerberg may not understand a thing about dwelling in God's presence, yet he birthed Facebook. He has been able to discover the due process of God though he is not a Christian.

UNDERSTAND GOD'S LAW ON THE EARTH

You live in a physical world and you must understand the physical laws and the material laws that God has put in place to guide it. If you do not know how to convert into physical tangible things, you will be of no benefit to anyone on earth, rather you will be a burden.

Pray as you want, be holier than angel Michael, prophesy till eternity, it will be of no benefit unless they are converted to benefit humanity. This is a physical world and the world must become flesh. When the world becomes flesh, it begins to benefit the world.

My dear friend, if you read the Bible so well but have not studied the subject of aeronautics, you cannot invent a plane no matter how badly you want. I'm just so sorry.

It gets an unbeliever much more pain, yet they stick with it. A Christian has the ideas every day through inspiration but fail to convert due to a poor mind.

The Bible says God spoke once and twice I have heard that power belongs to God. When God speaks it is like a wave, it keeps reverberating that people continue to hear it, even to the end of the earth. God releases his spirit and it depends on whoever gets it.

Just like you when God has placed certain things on your mind, when you get elsewhere, you discover certain other people are already working on that same idea. When you fail to convert ideas, another person is receiving same idea and inspiration and is probably working on it. Many people are getting same idea you have on your mind, it depends on how fast you are to receiving it.

God will always release his ideas into open space, a few individuals will be able to capture it in the mind. That is how photography works, it is like photography.

Many cannot translate what they are inspired by into real life products and results. They talk all the time about the inspiration and make lots of noise quoting the scriptures, yet there is no fruit. Nothing tangible to see or behold.

DON'T JUST READ THE BIBLE

When Pastors tell their members to read just the Bible, it is the greatest disservice to them. We make people irrelevant when we tell them not to read other books. We waste people when we tell them to come to church every day without sitting in their labs. Engineers won't be able to come up with original ideas, Doctors will have no leading thoughts, and you cannot change media or commerce. Information technology and medicine will lack substantive ideas. When the mind is not developed in these spheres, other people will leave you behind and you become irrelevant.

This is the understanding that Jews have. They have more Nobel Prize winners on earth. They connect to inspiration and they have been able to convert their ideas. They constantly and consistently release breath-taking inventions.

At least 197 Jews and people of Jewish ancestry have been awarded the Nobel Prize, this is out of the total 911 people who have been awarded the prize till 2016. This accounts for 22% of all individual recipients worldwide between 1901 and 2016. You will appreciate this statistic better when you understand that Jews currently make up approximately 0.2% of the world's entire population.

In Chemistry (36 prize winners alone are Jews, 21% of total prize winners in this category)

In Economics (30 prize winners alone are Jews, 38% of total Prize winners in this category)

In Physics (52 prize winners alone are Jews, 26% of total Prize winners in this category)

In Physiology or Medicine (55 prize winners alone in this category are Jews).

This is a direct contrast to the total Nobel Prize winners that have come from Africa. Can you guess how many Nobel Prize winners the whole of Africa of more than 1.2 billion people have produced since inception of the award? The result is shocking, just 10 people.

The Jews alone, with population of about 6 million people all over the world have produced almost twenty times more Prize winners than the whole continent of Africa.

What am I saying? We all can be as smart as Daniel if we study the wisdom of Babylon as well as the wisdom Of Israel. If we study the wisdom of God and implement the wisdom of whatever subject we choose to study.

When we combine the knowledge of our campuses and colleges with the wisdom from the word of God, we simply become unbeatable. We raise next set of Steve Jobs, Bill Gates and the next rulers of the world.

Only by the same way can we get the testimony that Joseph got, he combined the wisdom of Egypt with the wisdom of knowledge of God. He became unmatchable. His mind was trained and developed. He was so good that the men of the land could not match him.

Both men, that is Daniel and Joseph could not be matched in secrets and knowledge of their own kings. They had more understanding than those who taught them.

I PAID THE PRICE

When I first came to Russia from Nigeria, the school was already long in session. I arrived so late and ill prepared that one of my professors who was an atheist at the time told me it would never be possible for me to learn the language. According to him, it would be easier for him to believe in God and go to Church to light a candle than to believe I could pass. I took it as a challenge and began studying in the library for at least six hours every day. That began a lifelong culture of learning for me. At the end of the year, I did not just become the best, I was able to set an academic record in the school which has remained unbeaten for many years. I passed not because I was praying and sitting in Church all day, I passed and set a record because I sought to develop my mind.

You do not learn a language by praying and studying the Bible, you do not make ground breaking discoveries in science by fasting. You have to pay the price of work and study.

If we combine prayer with work and study, the knowledge of God and of Babylon, we will change the world. What Steve Jobs, Bill Gates and Mark Zuckerberg have achieved will seem too small.

The only way Joseph could preserve the food of Egypt for 7 years through a super refrigeration system was because he had insight. He did not just have interpretation of dreams, God knew he had the know-how in math, Physics and technology to store food for 7 years that would last the entire world. He was chosen because he was prepared. That was simply incredible.

He did not wake up with such knowledge suddenly in one day, he took time to develop his mind through prison and the years in Potiphar's house. His mind was so prepared the wise men of Egypt could not compare. Joseph studied the best wisdom Of Egypt combined with the best wisdom of God.

If you choose to do this, there will be no one comparable to you when it comes to releasing beneficial products than anyone else in the world.

Daniel was so disciplined to learn the wisdom of Babylon and he got everything necessary until he became the best. He added this wisdom to the knowledge of Israel he already had. He did this so consistently he was found to be 10 times better than the sons of the land. Such a man is unstoppable. He became the prime minister in a foreign land.

If you must convert your spiritual experiences into tangible products, your mind cannot be void. I just released unto you the secret.

You must always remember that all the things you feel when you pray and read the Bible and go to church are needed and necessary. They are the energy that is needed. You must learn to make sure your mind is ready to receive something new. With that frequency of God's spirit moving upon your spirit, it births inspiration and with a connected mind, the idea comes. Though it comes as a word, a thought or a seed, it is potent enough to change the world.

GOLDEN NUGGETS
FROM CHAPTER 1

- The things that have been created and the things that do not yet exist are all energy.

- The first thing that must be done for invisible energy to become tangible product is that we need inspiration.

- The best way to respond is to learn to convert inspiration and frequency into products.

- In God's presence, his spirit begins to interact with our spirit to deal with every darkness and emptiness of life.

- When you sing in worship and you are in praise, you must immediately begin to convert your experience into IDEAS.

- The level to which your mind is already developed determines the depth and extent of answers that it can bring about.

- The end point of inspiration must not just be mere words, but also thoughts and ideas.

- The mind must be developed, everything depends on how well you have developed your mind.

- Even if you are the holiest of holiest persons, you will be useless on the earth if your mind has not been developed.

CHAPTER 2

WISDOM ON CONVERTING INVISIBLE ENERGY TO TANGIBLE PRODUCTS

In this chapter, we are going to focus on how to convert your ideas into tangible products. The world does not thrive on ideas but products. No one uses ideas to cook or to clean, we use products. The question now is how do you transform your ideas into products?

Let us consider a few principles that will guide you in this process. Like you already understand that principles are universal. Principles do not work for you because of your race, background or religion. Principles work because you obeyed them. For you to be of benefit on earth, you must learn the principles of converting an idea from the invisible world into tangible products. You must gain knowledge of turning your spirituality, prayers and Bible reading into the physical, tangible forms. If you will be relevant on this side of eternity, you must convert your relationship with God into something visible. You must dare to convert your love into something physical, to convert prophecy into manifestation, to convert kindness into something tangible.

ENERGY MUST BE CONVERTED

Like I said previously, everything is energy. Energy cannot be created nor destroyed. Since everything is energy, it must be converted into other forms. Your ideas can be converted into money. Your inspiration can be converted into resources. In fact, all ideas must be converted into something tangible, into material products.

How do you convert all the wonderful ideas and inspiration you have always had into valuable substances. How do you bring substances from the intangible into the tangible?

In order to become successful in anything and to bring God's glory in everything, you have to learn the secret of conversion.

CREATE MENTAL PICTURES OF YOUR IDEA

Now in order to be able to convert your invisible resources; time, character, virtues, ideas, prayers etc you must pay attention to a very special word. This word is essential for conversion to ever happen or take place. The word is called PICTURE. It is a word I'm sure you are already familiar with. Picture is essential and fundamental if you must truly convert.

Remember that we are trying to learn how to convert intangible into tangible things, we are learning how to convert invisible energy into products. The most important word in conversion is pictures. Why is that? How come pictures?

Earlier in this book, you read about the process of inspiration and giving birth to ideas. Now that you have an idea, you need pictures of that thing that you are willing to convert. After gaining an understanding of your idea, you must create pictures in your mind. From understanding comes pictures. Before anything becomes tangible, it will first exist as a picture in your mind.

Let me use an illustration from the Bible. Proverbs 24: 3-5 states,

"By wisdom a house is built, and by understanding it is established; by knowledge the rooms are filled with all precious and pleasant riches. A wise man is full of strength, and a man of knowledge enhances his might."

Solomon the smartest man that ever lived knows something about this subject we are talking about. About building, he said, 'through wisdom a house is built'.

How could you build a house through wisdom? Wisdom itself is intangible. So how come something tangible can come out from something as intangible as wisdom?

That is exactly what God did and that is how he does it. Everything that God created and that we see now came out of the intangible.

The next line then stated, *'By understanding it is established.'*

This is really deep. How do you understand that? This is talking about conversion. I already stated that the most important word you will ever learn in your life is CON-

VERSION. When it comes to your existence on earth this conversion is essential. That's what that passage is about.

Every house that you see, everything that is built is built by wisdom. A country is built by wisdom, nations are built by wisdom, technologies are built by wisdom, industries are built by wisdom, economies are built by wisdom, successful political careers are built by wisdom, sons are built by wisdom, families are built by wisdom. Everything built and that exists came forth as an offspring of wisdom. Everything functional came forth from wisdom.

BUILDING BY WISDOM

Now, how do you understand and how do you glean wisdom from understanding? What does Solomon mean? For you to know what Solomon is talking about, you must know what wisdom is. Wisdom is the power, source and energy, the skill, craft and the ability that makes things built.

What therefore is wisdom? Wisdom is the ability to see what God sees and how God sees it. The elementary and fundamental aspect of that definition is that wisdom exists for building. The real understanding of wisdom is the ability to see, not with the physical eyes but with the mental eyes. Wisdom also is the ability to see with the eyes of the mind and to paint pictures, mental pictures. In summary, wisdom is pictures in the mind. Wisdom therefore is crucial.

Let me bring this closer home, how does this apply to you? Through wisdom and mental pictures, you can build anything you want to build in life.

Let's take this book in your hand as an example, what Solomon is saying is that this book was built twice.

The first time a house is built is by wisdom. It is first built in the mind of the architect. Anything that is of worth and quality that is built, it has to be built in the mind of somebody first.

Even in our world, God had to see the light first in his mind before he declared 'Let there be light'. Because he saw all that first in his mind, he could declare later that it was good. He had seen light, grass, animals, trees, all bacteria etc first in the mind.

The ability to create the picture of what you want in your mind is what is called wisdom. Wisdom sees the invisible. What is still invisible to everything and everyone else, a man of wisdom is already seeing it and already carrying it around.

Therefore, the second time that a house is built is by wisdom. This has everything to do with the details aspect. In the house where you are now, before the land was gotten, you probably had the plan drawn by an architect. The land might still be a jungle but the architect was seeing pictures already.

The concept and pictures in his mind made him draw them into papers. He downloaded them from his mind into a sheet of paper. At that stage it is almost concluded, it was just a matter of time. At that stage you could envision the rooms, you could see the walls, and you could walk the floors in your mind and it is just a question of time for it to be brought forth into the physical.

The understanding aspect is what the masonry and brick layers built.

It is same thing with family, if you have to build a successful family entity, you need first the pictures in your mind. If you want to build the country, you need pictures. If you do not have pictures, you will mess up the process.

Anything you want to construct in life must first be constructed in your mind.

To convert any invisible concept you have or any invisible energy, you need pictures. You must create energy into ideas and from an idea you must create pictures. From an idea, thought or word, you must create a picture of what you got or what you see.

How do you create pictures from an idea? Let's look into that more critically.

Let's say you do not understand the Russian language and you suddenly in the place of prayers got the word 'Yablaka'. Let's say God told you further that Yablaka will make you a millionaire. Let's say you got a word to go start an industry or business on Yablaka and in one year, Yablaka will make you a millionaire. So go do it.

Let's also say that I said to you, bring me one Yablaka or bring me some of it. At least you have to get hold of one or see it before you can mass produce it.

Now if you do not know the Russian language, you probably do not know the word Yablaka and have no idea of what it means. You could think it means a lot more other things that have no relevance to the original word.

You cannot picture Yablaka because you have not learnt the Russian language. Pictures will be impossible or extremely difficult when the information has not become stored in the mind. And anything that you are unable to picture, you cannot create. That is what Solomon meant when he said a house is built by wisdom. A house is built not just by vision but by exact pictures in the mind. Visions could be mere goals but pictures are definite. Without pictures, your mind cannot fathom it, if you cannot get the pictures, you cannot birth it.

Many Christians take the Bible, read the Bible and study the Bible. Many more people pray the Bible and confess the Bible and can preach and teach the Bible but have not been able to form pictures of the Bible. The word of God becomes transformational when pictures of what we read are formed in the mind. That is why we have not been creative and inventive. That is why Steve Jobs and Bill Gates are lacking in Church. That is why we are not captains of industries, inventors and leading researchers. We read the Bible as mere religion and for the goose bumps experience, not to derive pictures. Only things that you can make tangible benefit the world.

This is the lesson that Solomon is passing across, and Solomon is only saying again what God did in Genesis when he was creating all of creation.

GOD'S STRATEGY IS PUTTING PICTURES IN OUR MIND

God told Abraham, I will make you father of nations. Abraham asked how this will happen. God told him that he will make his descendants like the sand of the seashore. God was trying to paint a picture and engrave it in his mind. He said 'like the sand of the seashore'.

Only when you see pictures can you bring it to tangibility.

God told him to get out of his easy chair, to walk through the night, to raise his eyes to the sky. God then asked Abraham, 'What do you see? He responded that he could see stars. God told him that if he could not count them, so will he not be able to count his descendants.

God had to make him grasp the pictures before he could handle it in real life.

MIND YOUR MIND

Pictures are formed in the mind, the mind creates pictures. With the mind, all imagination is made. That is again why your mind is your greatest possession on the earth. Your mind determines your effectiveness in life, it determines your relevance on earth. The more you develop your mind, the more successful you become on the earth.

When you go to churches where you are not allowed to read and study and do research, you know you have to run from such places as if it's a leprosarium. Nothing is of more importance that you possess than your mind.

In our illustration of the Yablaka, let's imagine you have no idea of the word Yablaka, though you might make some progress, you cannot make any significant progress. The person who will make the most progress is someone who has the total picture of what Yablaka means.

Another example is if I ask you to bring a book, you could bring a poorly printed book whereas someone else could bring a more colorful book because he has better pictures in his mind.

THE DETAILS ARE IN THE PICTURES

The pictures bring about the details, the details is what brings out the color, the radiance and the beauty.

When the architect designed my house initially, it was not attractive to me, but when he gave out the details it was unbelievable to me. I could see the color of every room, I could see each floor and the color of every wall. I could see the parking space, the tiles and I even imagined the furniture, the curtains, the window blinds, the kitchen etc. Everything came out of the pictures to me. It was irresistible, my mind burnt with the idea of the house both night and day. Details are that powerful.

You must see pictures, you must see details. Those details create and give you excellence.

I come from Nigeria and there is a particular food that is loved and often consumed for breakfast. As a matter of fact, I sold this growing up in my native land as a teenager. Now, let's assume you are American or European and God says the whole of Africa eats something for breakfast and he wants you to create an industry that creates this product in seconds. An industry that makes the best of it and that is capable of feeding millions of people and making you a billionaire. Let's say God says to you further that if you are able to make the right machinery for it, you will liberate many young people from joblessness and create food for the poor. That product is called 'Ogi'. That was what I made and produced as a teenager.

As an European, you might be able to pronounce it, read and memorize it, but if you cannot picture it, you will never be able to produce it.

It is same thing with Yablaka and every other thing and invention on earth.

The bottom line is this, whatever you are not able to picture you cannot produce.

In spite of God's love for you, in spite of the spirit filling, in spite of your ability to speak in tongues, in spite of praying, if you cannot form mental pictures, you cannot produce a single thing. This is the reason why many people die barren, fruitless and incapable of making a mark.

HOW TO GET A DETAILED PICTURE

Sometimes to get a detailed picture, you need to embark on research to make sure all the process is considered and all the factors are taken into account. Research helps you form the best picture and put all the different pieces together.

That's why Jesus often say, take heed of what you hear and see. You need to see in order to create pictures. The purpose of seeing is pictures and the end purpose of hearing is pictures. The end purpose therefore of information and all that we gather in preaching and teaching must be mental pictures. Otherwise it all becomes exercise in futility. The reason we seem to get little from all the preaching, sermons, teachings, vigils etc is because we have not been taught that the end product of information is pictures.

It is also the reason many go to school to acquire knowledge and information. Many graduates of colleges and universities cannot produce a thing because they cannot build mental pictures. If we are to build modern technology and inventions, modern railways and submarines. If we are to get the best of agriculture and medicine, if we are to build for the future and create a modern world for our children and children's children, if we are to partake in building the next world, then we must be able to form pictures in our mind.

A place where this teaching is needed urgently is in our schools and colleges in Nigeria. Statistics has reported that more than 500,000 students graduate from our higher institutions every year with about 200,000 of them being from the Universities. There is every probability that much more students than the quoted number graduate from our institutions.

Where are the mental pictures of all these people? Where are the results of their going to school? If every one of these graduates choose to dedicate himself to solving just one problem through the power of self-development and forming mental pictures, no doubt there will not be a single problem left to tackle again in Nigeria today.

Proverbs 4:7 says to us *"Wisdom is the principal thing; therefore get wisdom: and with all thy getting get understanding."*

Wisdom is key, wisdom is supreme, wisdom is of utmost importance, wisdom is the principal thing.

Based on this knowledge of scripture you had before? What does it mean to you now? Do you now understand what this means. Do you now see that your entire existence will be a waste on earth if you do not have wisdom?

Wisdom gives you the clear picture of planning. The reason why wisdom is the principal thing is that with wisdom you are able to build a clear picture. Through wisdom you create pictures, through wisdom you build. Wisdom gives you the picture and that is why wisdom is needed before anything comes to creation and is established. Picture is principal because wisdom is above all things, wisdom is principal because pictures are critical and necessary. Wisdom makes you create pictures in your mind. If you can see it you can do it. Wisdom is the main thing, it is the first thing. Through wisdom, the foundation of any building is laid.

When the architect draws the plan of the house, that is the wisdom part. The understanding part is what the physical builders lay out. Therefore we can say that the real building is done by wisdom or through the mental pictures.

What do you think? Which is more important, the work of the builders or the work of the architect? Of course, that of the architect. The architect does 75% of the work.

The ability to build pictures in your mind through pictures and in color through research and have every detail in place is 75% of what is needed to build unusual things on earth.

Once the design is ready, the physical construction of that idea is only 25%.

Before you must do anything, you need to first sit down and build the whole thing first through wisdom before you finish the remaining 25%.

Let us consider another illustration. Jesus said in Luke 14:28 *"Suppose one of you wants to build a tower. Won't you first sit down and estimate the cost to see if you have enough money to complete it?"*

Jesus was saying your success is dependent on your picturing. Don't rush. What many people do is to get an idea and start building immediately. We fail when we begin with the 25%. Jesus is saying, use wisdom to build. Don't use hands or legs, use wisdom. Sit down first, get the picturing correctly, in colors and in details. Once this is done, you can then proceed with the 25% of the work. If you want to go to war with a king, the system is the same or you come back defeated. Build systems, draw the plans, put structures in place and finish the house first. Often the work gets done without any further challenges.

SELL EVERYTHING, ACQUIRE MENTAL PICTURES

Solomon had come to the extent when he could say sell everything that you have to acquire wisdom, to acquire that ability to see and picturize and envision.

The ultimate wisdom and source of it is the ability to see what God sees and connect your mind to his mind.

Wisdom therefore is ultimate when we can gain access and paint pictures of what God is trying to pass across to influence the earth.

Any idea, anything spiritual could be conceptualized into raw forms. Kindness, love, faith can all be converted. If you have kindness for example, sit down and make your calculations. Who do you want to show your kindness to, to whom do you want to be kind? Who needs your love? How much does it cost? What about partners and sponsors? Build these systems first. When this is done, it becomes very explosive and it reaches every part of the earth. Fame, feasibility and tangibility are all results of planning. Love can be converted through same process of picturing. It must be built, it must be planned, it must be worked out. You must be able to build a system for that love. Same thing with building a business, church or country. It works by pictures. By the way if you are still wondering, Yablaka means apple.

The point of everything is the power that exists in forming pictures.

Now Proverbs 8:12-15 makes more meaning now, when the bible says

"I, wisdom, dwell with prudence, and find out knowledge and discretion. The fear of the Lord is to hate evil; Pride and arrogance and the evil way and the perverse mouth I hate. Counsel is mine, and sound wisdom; I am understanding, I have strength. By me kings reign, and rulers decree justice."

EMBARK ON BEING PRUDENT

For you to be able to paint a picture, you must get knowledge and do research. Wisdom is a result of prudence, knowledge and information. And the process of converting that information into a picture is prudence. Without converting that knowledge into pictures, you will never be able to convert those information into pictures. Without that you will never be remarkably special or leave your steps in time.

Each time you read the Bible, turn what you read into pictures.

Once you go to pray, ensure that the goosebumps and the anointing you feel become ideas and the ideas become pictures. With these there is nothing you do that will not be exceptional. There is nothing you endeavor in that you will not be the best. This strategy is to make Christians the head everywhere. These are the strategies for Christians to rise again to be the leaders everywhere in business, in commerce, in industry, in government, in politics etc.

This is combining the wisdom of the Bible, wisdom of the world to overtake all the sons of the land. This is a call to be competitive, to overtake men and women like Steve jobs, Bill Gates, Richard Branson, Oprah Winfrey etc.

STOP BEING RELIGIOUS

We must stop being religious, unfortunately churches have been dishing religion out to people over the years. We read the Bible religiously, pray religiously and congregate religiously. We do things just for the goal of keeping routine and not for effectiveness. We seem to be addicted to our ineffective lifestyle. We are so ignorant and walk around with a full head, yet nothing about conversion. The only conversion many Christians know is the conversion from sin, nothing else.

By the time we make our Christianity convertible, and not just a matter of culture, then we will become world changers. The whole of the Bible is about making invisible things visible. All of the Bible is about conversion. The word of God became Jesus, the love of God had to be manifested for men to see. That is conversion.

The word about the Son of God, the baby Jesus being taken to Egypt came to pass in the physical realm.

The prophecy about Herod seeking after the life of the baby Jesus came to pass in the physical realm.

Simeon the devout who waited for the consolation of Israel through the birth of the Messiah saw his dream come to pass in the physical realm.

Hannah the prophetess who was a widow 7 years from her virginity who waited and did not depart from the temple to see the birth of the Messiah, saw her revelation come to pass in the physical realm.

The word that was given to Zachariah the father of John the Baptist came to pass in the physical realm.

Mary actually witnessed a physical manifestation of the word that was given her that Elizabeth was pregnant just like it was spoken to her.

The prophecy of Agabus that Paul was going to be in bondage in Jerusalem came to pass in the physical realm.

The word that Jesus would save people from their sins came to pass in the physical realm.

Jesus prophesied that this gospel will be preached to the ends of the earth, we are witnessing that prophecy today in the physical realm.

Jesus prophesied the coming of The Holy Spirit on the day of Pentecost and it came to pass physically.

Jesus spoke about the destruction of Jerusalem and it came to pass 70 years later.

Jesus prophesied His death and resurrection on the third day and it came to pass.

Friends, the point I am trying to make is that all these prophesies and words from the Lord, actually began in men's spirit as a thought, which later moved to their minds as ideas. But if the process had only stopped at the stage of thoughts or ideas, it wouldn't have been of benefit or blessings to the world.

> *Ideas are easy. It's the execution of ideas that really separates the sheep from the goats.*
>
> SUE GRAFTON

Anything that is not converted is not needed on the earth. Whatever exists as mere prayers and prophecies only are not beneficial.

All of your ideas are a waste if they cannot be converted, that is why the most important word to learn in your lifetime is the word conversion. If you are able to learn and master this act, then you will be unstoppable and you will become the best in your lifetime. Congratulations that you came across an information such as this and you came acr oss my book.

If you get this idea and concept right, you will become one of the most effective and successful people on the earth.

GOLDEN NUGGETS
FROM CHAPTER 2

- The world does not thrive on ideas but products.

- The most important word in conversion is pictures.

- The word of God becomes transformational when pictures of what we read are formed in the mind.

- Your mind determines your effectiveness in life, it determines your relevance on earth.

- The pictures bring about the details, the details is what brings out the color, the radiance and the beauty.

- Anything that you are unable to picture, you cannot create.

CHAPTER 3

YOU CAN BECOME AN INVENTOR, INNOVATOR AND A CO-CREATOR WITH GOD

Invention... and imitation, are the two legs, so to call them, on which the human race historically has walked.

WILLIAM JAMES

Overtime I have discovered some very interesting principles of life. I have discovered that all men are equal before God and in life. The reason many are inspired in life and seem to daily invent products, while others sit on the back bench of life is not farfetched. There are master-classes I have developed where I make people sit down and I instruct them on these principles. The results are amazing. A lot of people sit in these classes and we invent things right there in the class. Whatsoever God teaches me, I like to teach others and make them practice it. When God told me that I could become a millionaire I was curious about it. I thought of how I could produce other millionaires, and I produced 200 millionaires in two years. When I discovered that I could become a millionaire, I thought of how to produce other leaders too. I have produced over ten thousand leaders around the world working about everything. When I began to invent and innovate, I thought of also getting people who can innovate and invent. This chapter is all about these principles. You are going to learn so fast how to become an inventor in the order of Bill Gates and Steve Jobs and several other men that our world celebrate today.

EVERYONE CAN BECOME AN INVENTOR

Everybody can become an innovator and an inventor if they can have imagination and if they can work. If people can work mentally and add values to themselves, they can invent. If you can learn how to add values to product and services, if you can learn how to work hard, there is nothing you cannot become, there is nothing you cannot do.

One of the greatest revelations of my life, which I never knew is that life is predictable. I believe many people also do not know it. I always thought (and this school of thought is widespread all over the world) that life was not predictable, rather I used to think that life was a mystery. Many people still believe great men are lucky and that only few people are born to be great. Some people think greatness is a function of color, race or background. No, that is not true at all.

If I who was born in a village of less than forty houses could rise above obscurity. If I who came from a family that no one would otherwise talk about could become a star based on these principles that I have discovered, then you can too.

Men like Steve Jobs and Bill Gates were also ordinary men who had basically no background, no platform for greatness. They were men who no one believed in. But they discovered certain things that made them who they became. If you will understand and apply these same principles, you will also get same results and achieve much more than what you have achieved.

You see now dear friend that becoming an inventor is not whether you studied sciences or arts, it is not whether you were born in Nigeria or in Canada, it is whether you have discovered the laws that govern invention and innovation for yourself.

LIFE IS PREDICTABLE

Life is predictable. Yes, you probably have not heard that or you do not know that before. However, if you must become an inventor and innovator, then you must understand that life is predictable. Some other people say that we cannot control things, that belief is called fatalism. Fatalism is the belief that all events are predetermined and therefore inevitable. Others say that life is about luck and chance, but that is not true, instead life is predictable.

One of the ways by which life could be predictable is through hard work. One of the greatest discoveries of life for me is that life could be predictable and I can determine my future through the instrument of work. It is a major discovery that I could plan out my life. The saying that life is predictable is unbelievable for many people. I am going to give you some principles that makes life predictable and that will be able to help you predict and plan your life so that you can become an innovator, an inventor and a co-creator with God.

EVERY ACHIEVEMENT CAN BE REPEATED

The number one principle that is critical for you to understand is that you can replicate anything that has ever been done on the earth before. Any person that is willing can actually repeat any feat, any achievement especially to a greater degree. This means if anyone on this earth has ever become an inventor before, you can make up your mind to become an inventor and you will be. If it has been done before, it can be done again. If it has been achieved before, it can be easily repeated by anyone. You must not forget this. This also means that you can become the architect of your life and destiny. So that is one point that you must hold dear and must not forget. If there is anyone that you have read about or who truly inspires you, the good news is, that person is a human being like you. By this I mean if a living or dead human being like you could do it, you can repeat what the person has done before. When you read about men like Steve Jobs and Bill Gates, you know you can become like such men and reproduce those men in yourself.

WHAT IS HINDERING YOU IS
WHAT YOU DON'T KNOW

Another critical factor to note is that the only reason why people do not become anything they want to become is in what they have not discovered. It is in what they do not know yet. It is either this people do not understand the principles and laws used by that person or they are totally ignorant of them. The only reason why a person could fail or not achieve what he wants to achieve in life is because the person does not know certain things. That is a big missing link. This is why the bible says 'my people are destroyed because of lack of knowledge"(Hosea 4 vs. 6).

If you could discover the principles, laws, rules that other people used to become who they are, then you stand the great chance of being able to do the same thing. Many people are not able to do what they want to do in life. A lot of people fail to become what they want to become (which either anyone in the world has succeeded in becoming or not). The reason is that such people have not known the secrets they ought to know in other to achieve the feat. The overarching reason is that such individuals may not have the same purpose that others have. All the time, you have to go through the same process that others have gone through to become who they became.

You must also discover the discipline and the tenacity to go through that process. Though you know all the laws and rules, you cannot become significant if you are not able to undergo the discipline that life requires. Unless you are willing to go through the process that others went through, you will not be able to become what you want to become.

Life is predictable. Whatsoever your name is, wherever you are right now, irrespective of who your parents were or even if you never had parents, you can become anything you wish to become including becoming an inventor. An innovator is a co-creator with God. If someone has done it before, then it makes it easier for you to become and for you to do it also. Whatsoever people have done before can be repeated.

The next essential step that is needed is to master the principles, laws that other people have used before. The third step is your willingness and discipline. Are you ready to pay the price and what it takes to go through the process? How ready are you to endure the pain of going through the process?

WHAT ABOUT THE HINDERANCES?

Right now you are probably thinking about the hindrances you are going to encounter and the likely obstacles? You are probably thinking about hindrances that can be posed by unseen circumstances and some forces.

There are ways and strategies that can be used to overcome these forces and circumstances. If you have the willingness to pay the price and become disciplined, life becomes predictable. The decision to stay true is the ultimate. It is exciting news for me to know that I can set my life in motion; I can become the architect of my life. When I discovered this, I began to build a system for my life, I started to live my life twenty years forward. With proper planning, any obstacle and hindrance can be overcome.

For example, if I am fifty years old now, I look into what I will be at seventy and start from now to build. I begin to live with the next twenty years of my life in view. I am currently living a life planned out for the next three hundred years because I have discovered that I can plan my life three hundred years ahead. Even when I am dead physically, when I am no more here on earth, I will still be alive in the next three hundred years. I am working for the success of the next three hundred years.

HOW TO BECOME A CO-CREATOR WITH GOD

You can become an inventor, you too can become an innovator and you too can become a co-creator with God. The most beautiful part of it is that it is quite easy. Everyone can become an inventor because the inventor gene and ability is living inside every one of us. God is a creator. This is the greatest key for every one of us to become a continuous creator. God, the continuous inventor is inside of us, and we have the mind of Christ. That God is in us, makes it a reality. The nature of God is in us, so we are co-creators with God. The very best and the greatest inventor is within us, the inventor gene lives inside of us because we are made in His image.

If He is a creator and makes you in His image, then who are you? He is the ultimate creator and He created you just to become like him, then what is your excuse? It means that the ability to create is buried inside of you. This is why mental work or mental labor is the most potent form of work a person can do. That is why you could become all that you were born to be through work. History makers work through their brain. History makers are thinkers. History makers are builders. Through your brain, you are simply bringing forth what already lies buried within you.

BECOME AN INVENTOR THROUGH WORK

Though this very vital point will be discussed in greater details in a later chapter, I must emphasize at this point that the instrumentality through which God wants to release His creative ability in us is through work. Because you already have the nature of an inventor living in you. The supreme innovator is in you, there is no doubt that the inventing and creating ability of God is in you. It is in your particles, in your cells, in your molecule. All your molecules and cells are calling out that you have the nature of God in you. The ability of God is within you.

We have been deceived that we cannot do the extra-ordinary, we have been made to believe that we are not supernatural, and that we cannot do all things. We have been deceived that only the geniuses can become inventors and create things. We have been deceived that some people have the talent while we do not have the talent. We have been deceived that only some people have the ability and that we all do not have the ability. We have been deceived that we are not capable. We have been deceived that all we need do is just go to work for someone, many are living for just the job that they do. We have been deceived that we should just go and get a salary. Oh no! The DNA of God is in you. Because the DNA of God is in you, you can unveil the nature of God within you. You can unveil the nature of an inventor in yourself. You can unveil God's nature in yourself by going to the laboratory and challenging your mind.

You need to get into thinking and reading, because it is only the things that you put in yourself that you can get out of yourself. If you don't put knowledge and innovation into yourself, you will not be able to bring things out for yourself. If you do not put knowledge, innovation, and know-how into yourself, you will never be able to bring it out of yourself. You must put into yourself some knowledge and innovations. You must be able to study and push yourself hard. You must be able to push yourself and go deep.

You must get yourself engaged, not in some television show series, not in some Hollywood or Nollywood movies. If Hollywood and Nollywood are the only things you engage your mind with, you will never invent anything because your mind is already filled with pictures of other people. When your mind is filled with the pictures of other people you will not be able to bring out the picture that God has put inside of you. There are pictures that are buried in your mind. This is what I have demonstrated with my personal life and this is what I have taught people over the years.

Right now, you must discover how to become an innovator and an inventor. In my master-classes which I have held for several years in my adopted country of Ukraine, several hundreds of people have become inventors. Many people have become inventors by applying these principles and many other principles that will be revealed to you in this book. You will discover that you can invent something, especially that which you have always had in mind to do. Every cell in your body right now is carrying an invention that will shake the world. When you are done with this book, you will start coming up with several inventions, you will be amazed at your products. You too can become an inventor. You need to challenge what is inside of you to arise and the way to challenge it is through hard work.

Through hard work we can reveal the inventor in us. Through hard work, we reveal, discover, and unveil the innovator in us. Through hard-work we discover all the hidden inventions that are in ourselves. There are some things in you so unique to yourself and that are hidden in you by God. They are your inventions.

YOU HAVE BEEN AN INVENTOR ALL YOUR LIFE

In order to press on this issue of innovating and inventing further, I will like to tell you something very interesting. Do you know you have been an inventor all your life? You have been putting many things forth as inventions for a long time, you just fail to see it and realize it. You see, we are all inventing when we dress, when we use our makeups, when we combine colors as we dress, when we write stories or when we tell and share stories. We are all inventing every day, you only probably have not noticed it.

Right now, you only need to take that higher and believe God that He will use you to do greater things. Through your ability to invent, new things will come forth and things that eyes have not seen will be birthed. To become an inventor and an innovator is easier than what you think. Life is predictable through hard work, through mental work. Inventions come through hard work, mostly mental work. To discover the laws and principles that make people become who they are, you have to study and apply your mind. You must do self-study. If you can go through the discipline the other person that invented has gone through, nothing can stop you from becoming an inventor.

Pastors are not the only men of God; all of us are men of God because God is in all of us. If you will become anything in life, you have to learn to work for at least fourteen to eighteen hours a day. I am not talking about your job, but I am talking about working for your purpose and adding values to yourself. God created us in His image therefore we are co-creators with God.

HOW TO BECOME AN INVENTOR

How then do we become inventors? How do you generate ideas? How do you constantly rain down new products on the earth? Many people are amazed when I say that I write a new book every week. They just cannot fathom it, but that is true. Let me show you how you can also constantly generate new products that will continue to impact your generation.

Now the scriptures said that the invincibility of God is made visible by His works (the nature) that we can see. There is a great secret in this.

The key to invention and creation is nature. Everything God created is only a seed or a suggestion or an idea. It is a whisper. It is a seed, a picture for you. God is only making a recommendation to us by everything he made, his works are proposals for us to work on and thoroughly develop.

The source of innovation and invention is nature. Everything (including the sky) we see is a shadow. Behind them are many more ideas. Everything we see is just an intuition, a prototype, an idea, a suggestion. Everything you see all around you now is just a tip of the iceberg. Look at the cloth you are wearing right now, it comes from nature. The food you ate today came from nature. Everything comes from nature, so the very thing you need to know about creativity and innovation is an idea.

The whole of nature is a hint for us through which we can get our own idea or several other ideas. Everything we observe in all of nature is an idea. If we can study any nature in details, if we could think, then everything we study in nature and observe carefully will give birth to new ideas for us. This is why you need a lot of time to study and observe.

For example, for the production of my cloth, somebody looked at nature and patterns in nature to produce it. The design on your cloth could be a product of plant and animals as well. It might be inspired by the skin of snake and flowers. Your cloth is a production of innovation. You have your iPad and computers and it is now possible for you to watch me through them because somebody studied nature. What gave birth to computers and smart phones is that people began to study the mind and the brain of people. It is the study of man that gave birth to robots. The observation of flies and doves gave birth to the invention of planes. It was the speed of horse power, of animals that gave birth to the innovation, the invention and creativity that birthed cars. Everything that is produced is from nature. That is one idea that you must know.

NATURE BIRTHS ALL IDEAS

In order for me to illustrate this idea beautifully, and in order for you to understand what I am saying clearly, let us look at it in the Bible. The scriptures declared in Psalm 19 vs. 1-10.

¹ The heavens declare the glory of God;
The skies proclaim the work of his hands.
² Day after day they pour forth speech;
night after night they reveal knowledge.
³ They have no speech, they use no words;
no sound is heard from them.
⁴ Yet their voice goes out into all the earth,
their words to the ends of the world.
In the heavens God has pitched a tent for the sun.

⁵ It is like a bridegroom coming out of his chamber,
like a champion rejoicing to run his course.
⁶ It rises at one end of the heavens
and makes its circuit to the other;
nothing is deprived of its warmth.
⁷ The law of the Lord is perfect,
refreshing the soul.
The statutes of the Lord are trustworthy,
making wise the simple.
⁸ The precepts of the Lord are right,
giving joy to the heart.
The commands of the Lord are radiant,
giving light to the eyes.
⁹ The fear of the Lord is pure,
enduring forever.
The decrees of the Lord are firm,
and all of them are righteous.
¹⁰ They are more precious than gold,
than much pure gold;
they are sweeter than honey,
than honey from the honeycomb.

Many people look at the Bible as religious books, but it ought not to be looked at like that. The Bible should be seen as book of invention. The Bible is a book of ideas. You can look at the bible and see different things. The Bible will give you ideas and innovations. I want to show you how you can use the bible for innovation, inventions and become a co-creator with God. The primary instrument of invention is the nature. Nature makes the invisible visible, behind every visible thing that you see is the whole invisible world that is waiting to be discovered and expressed.

Hence the invisible God is seen through the visible creation. If you will look well, study well, research well, and if you challenge your mind well, the invisible God becomes visible to you by observing the acts of creation.

This tells us that if you want to invent or create any visible thing, just look critically at anything you like in nature. You need to begin to look at anything visible, behind them are a whole lot of invisible truths. A lot of invisible realities that you can bring to pass are hidden in nature. There is a lot that you can bring to life, there is a lot that you can birth on the earth. What has been created by God is a hint. The rest are hidden for the observant among us to discover. When God made trees and showed it to Adam, he was only giving him a hint for chairs, tables, furniture, boats and ships, housing etc.

So look around you now, what do you see from nature? What are the plants saying to you? Can you hear the insects? What can you see and hear? Can you hear anything at all?

The bible also tells us that everything that is visible is temporal, which means the just shall live by faith. The ability to look at something that is visible in order to see something that is invisible is the source of creation. Behind everything that is visible is something invisible. What has become visible is already temporal, it has become limited.

The invisible things are of more value, they are of more worth. This is why the bible says that the visible things are temporal. Faith is looking behind the visible things to see the invisible things, because the invisible things are eternal. The invisible things are the things that last, that is why the bible says that "the just shall live by faith." This means that the just shall live by the invisible things.

Faith is the substance of things hoped for and the evidence of things not seen. Now you can begin to see the word 'faith' in a new light. For me, one of the most misused words on earth is faith. A lot of people use it but do not understand it. We cannot say you have faith unless you are able to birth something visible on earth from the invisibility that exists in God's mind or in nature. The ability to look at things that are seen in order to see things that are invisible is called innovation. The ability to see and birth those invisible things is called Faith.

That is how innovation comes.

NATURE IS CRYING OUT TO YOU

Let me do some master-class for you here, I am sure this will change your life. Psalm 19 vs 1 says.

"The heavens declare the glory of God; And the firmament shows His handiwork."

Every time you look at the heaven, the skies and firmaments are speaking to you. Can you hear them? So also is every part of the nature. They have got a message for you, they are communicating to you right now. What are the trees saying to you? What are the flowers communicating? What is all of nature's words to you? Can you hear anything at all? What is the sun whispering to you? Can you hear anything at all?

The heavens are not just speaking to us, they are shouting and screaming out. The heavens are declaring, and only few are able to hear them. Nature is screaming, can you hear me?

How do you get to listen to what all of nature is saying to you? You discover what the heavens are speaking through hard work, through mental work and through careful observation.

There are three forms of labor; the physical labor (which is the least), the mental labor, and the spiritual labor. If you do enough spiritual work, you will begin to see and hear what the heavens are declaring.

Some scientists have developed their minds and have discovered that the heavens, the sky, the cosmos could be explored, the space could be explored. They started creating and bringing about things through constant studying, through developing their minds. What about if we could develop our own spirit.

Every day, the heavens are declaring things that humanity is supposed to discover. When we subdue the heavens, when we subdue the outer space, we bring glory to God. We do same when we bring the earth also under dominion. The same with the firmament which shows God's handiwork. What about the water bodies? Imagine the plants?

Think about the billions of insects that exist. They all are revealing something. When we look at the sky for example, we are supposed to be getting pictures and ideas in our mind. Many people love blue color because they look at the sky. This is the elementary form of it. Many observe the sky and see patterns and designs. The firmament, the skies are showing pictures.

It is foolish to let some people put you in a box and lock you up in some churches only for you to hear repeatedly that Jesus died. They tell you constantly that Jesus loves you, reciting about the cross of Jesus and praying against your enemies, basically wasting your time. Why should you let somebody waste your life when you only have one life? You only have a few years to go, you only have little time on earth. Even one hundred and twenty years is too small for you to exhaust all of what God has placed in you. Why don't you develop your mental prowess, your mental power and your spiritual power through hard work? Your increased capacity to catch and develop pictures. Why don't you learn to discover the firmaments, the sky? Why don't you learn to hear the heavens? Why don't you think about the language of birds and discover them. Why don't you see the wonders of the water waves and the whispering of the oceans?

Imagine the 51.6% of Nigerians who are Christians having this understanding and living with it, in no time we will not just conquer the entire country, we will also conquer the earth.

This is the Wisdom of Solomon, the wisest man that ever walked the surface of the earth. The Bible said about Solomon in 1 Kings 4:33

"He (Solomon) could speak with authority about all kinds of plants, from the great cedar of Lebanon to the tiny hyssop that grows from cracks in a wall. He could also speak about animals, birds, small creatures, and fish." What a depth? What a level of wisdom?

YOU CAN INVENT EVERYDAY

Verse two of Psalm 19 says: *"Day unto day utters speech, And night unto night reveals knowledge."*

These are the keys to invention. Everyday releases to you new inventions and innovations to us. Can you imagine that? The reason why you are able to read this book is because of pictures. You can see pictures on what would have otherwise been blank pages. Words appear as pictures in the pages of the book. This is what the bible is saying here. Every day there are new pictures that are released to the airwaves by nature, waiting on anyone to catch them. Right now, you could read from me through the mechanism of print media, it is possible for you to watch me via the internet, you can see me through computers as I release my picture into the air if you so wish. When you watch Television, you get tuned to the frequency and wave which gives you pictures. This is how the heavens and God are releasing ideas and inventions into the world every single day. Not only do they utter speech, everything speaks. You need to be able to hear what the mornings and evenings are speaking.

Only a trained mind has this capacity. You can only do this through a developed mind. This means simply everyday affords you an opportunity to invent. Through the millions of signals that is being given each day, you have no excuse not to become an inventor.

CONVERT NATURE INTO A LANGUAGE FOR ALL

There is no speech nor language where their voice is not heard.
PSALM 19:3

Imagine the different time zones in the world. It could be morning at a certain place, simultaneously it is also night in many other places. Night also speak. Nature is only communicating to every people and every language in a way that relates to them. Same with weather.

You need to work to get information and convert the information into valuable products and bless the world and glorify your father in heaven. You must convert what you have heard from nature into a language, into a form that all men can understand. God has equipped us with the needed raw materials for innovation and inventions. There is no speech and language where what nature is saying is not heard. When you have caught the information, it becomes a responsibility to convert the language of nature or what nature is saying into a language every man on earth can understand.

There is a man called George Washington Calver and that is a name you are going to come across often in this book. He is one of the greatest inventors of all time and one I personally admire.

The reason why I love George Washington Calver is because he taught me to be an inventor. So also is Steve Jobs, so also is Bill gates. Others are Thomas Edison, Nikolas Tesla etc. They taught me to become an inventor when I studied their lives. We don't have any excuse not to be extra-ordinary or supernatural or not to be a huge success.

George Washington Calver was just observing plants and trees. God gave him a hint into groundnut, and he produced over two thousand products from groundnut alone. He started studying potato and He made products from it, over 300 products that he made were recorded. Many people see potato as mere ingredients for breakfast. George Washington Calver saw much more. With his products, he was able to deliver an entire nation from economic mess.

Anything you make up your mind to study and discipline yourself to discover can make you explode in life in a big and positive way. Nature will speak to you in your own language. You will discover God in your own language. You will discover so many other things through any form of nature.

In nature God has set a tabernacle. We got electricity and other forms of energy from studying the sun. Nature is supposed to bring us to the discovery of God but we can't discover that without good research and analysis. Anywhere and anything you read in the bible is pregnant with inventions.

Can you now see that it is quite easy to become an inventor? I am sure that while reading these words, ideas are already running through your minds. Please write those ideas down right now. I will teach how to convert those energies and ideas into tangible products shortly in this book. From today, inspiration will begin to pour upon you like rainfall. Your life does not have to be dry and boring. Your place is among the giants in life. You can be among the next set of Steve Jobs and Bill Gates of your generation.

GOLDEN NUGGETS
FROM CHAPTER 3

- Everybody can become an innovator and an inventor if they can have imagination and if they can work.

- Life is predictable.

- You can replicate anything that has ever been done on the earth before.

- Unless you are willing to go through the process that other inventors went through, you will not be able to become what you want to become.

- The instrumentality through which God wants to release His creative ability in us is through work.

- You can become an inventor every day.

CHAPTER 4

HOW TO BECOME RELEVANT ON THE EARTH

One of the greatest battles any man will fight on earth is the battle for relevance.

Following the insights of the previous chapters in this book, we want to continue in the same vein. In this chapter, we will be learning why "spiritual experiences without conversion remains irrelevant", and how to make yourself a person of value and relevance in this world. If you have been reading this book carefully, and if you have followed carefully the line of thought, you will probably remember the language and the word that I said is the most important word you will ever learn in your life. The most important word you will ever learn in your life is the word "conversion."

Do you want to be a kingdom person and do you want to be relevant to the kingdom of God here on earth? Do you want to be relevant to heaven and to receive praise in heaven? Do you want to receive glory and crown in heaven?

Then you need to learn that word. The most important word you will ever learn on this side of the planet is the word "conversion." There is no word that is more important than that word. If you could master that word "conversion' you would have become one of the most dangerous human beings walking on the face of the earth.

If you will not just know the word "conversion" but if you will master it, if you will master conversion, if you could only learn and operate "conversion", you would have learnt the most important task and the most important assignment that God has for humanity. You would have also mastered the most important instrument and the most important key to effective living. That key is "conversion."

SPIRITUAL EXPERIENCES ARE NOT ENOUGH

Since we are Christians and we are people who want to be in the Spirit all the time, we are people who always want to have spiritual experiences. That is the reason the topic I am discussing extensively in this book is conversion. Spiritual experiences without conversion remain irrelevant and is empty religion. If you go to India or you go to some Asian countries you will see what evil religion is. If you go to Africa or you go to some idol worshipping, gentile or pagan celebrations, you will see the danger of religion. If you visit some paganist religious practices, you will see how horrible religion could be.

There is perhaps no nation on earth that presents ugly face of religion like India. In India, religion is put on a ped-

estal without any conversion and because of lack of conversion; you could see how evil religion could be. Religious
practices and religious experiences without conversion lead
human beings into devastation and waste. So here we go,
we who are Christians will end up repeating mistakes of
the religious practices of our world without conversion.

Furthermore, if you go to the Middle East as well and
you see Islam, it will also show you what religion could do
without conversion. As Christians we are not supposed to
be religious. We are not supposed to merely practice religion. We are supposed to practice a life with God. We are
supposed to have an experience with God and that experience should not give birth to the monster called religion.
The experience we have has to include in itself conversion.
That is why the most important word you could learn as a
Christian and as a human being is the word conversion.

I made my point clear to you earlier, I was able to communicate to you that the purpose of the entire word of God,
of the revelations of God, is for it to be converted. Again
I must say that anything that remains unconverted in the
spirit realm is a waste and does not benefit people on earth.

I am emphasizing another aspect of that instruction in
this chapter, I am saying all your spiritual experiences must
be converted. As Christians we like to have spiritual experiences, we love to experience prophecies etc. Some people
go to church just for prophecies, others go to church just for
worship experiences. So many people are in worship centers
for singing, worship etc. It is a waste to do all those things

just for goose bumps without converting them. When you do spiritual exercises to feel good and to feel high, without converting anything, then you have only engaged in spiritual stimulation without any benefit to humanity.

If you want your spiritual experiences to benefit humanity, and to benefit the kingdom of God on earth (not in heaven but on earth), those experiences, those revelations must also be converted. It is only when they are converted to physical, tangible goods that the people in the world will be able to see your light shining. It is only then they will be able to give glory to your father who is in heaven.

Everyone loves to be blessed. Everyone loves to talk about all kinds of blessings including spiritual blessings. You must however understand that anything that God is giving you in the Spirit must become products. Anything God is giving out to human beings will remain irrelevant if we don't convert them to products. All the blessings that God is giving you will remain irrelevant until they are converted. You might go into worship and have a wonderful spiritual experience, but if you don't get some information from that experience and know what to convert it into, it will remain irrelevant.

CONVERT THROUGH A DEVELOPED MIND

A lady who loves to sing and worship once wrote a letter to me. In the letter, she wrote of an experience she had while she was listening to one of my teachings. According to her, just by listening to that teaching, a lot of ideas began to come to her. Now this is what happened, she was listening to me and was being blessed and imparted spiritually by my words. The more significant thing was that my words were giving birth to ideas in her mind because she has already been prepared in the area of her calling. She is a film producer and song writer. She knew and had the skill already, she knows her trade. When the mind is not prepared, it does not matter what amount of anointing that is poured on a person, it will be in waste.

You see my dear friend, the mind that is not prepared will not fathom what God is trying to say. But when you feel the anointing of God, the inspiration of the spirit, the goose bumps, when you feel the touch of God, that is a sign to you that heaven is open upon you. When God is releasing some information, you should key in immediately into the Spirit realm and download some understanding.

So when you feel the Spirit of God, and feel the inspiration of his spirit, then it is time for action. When you feel the goose bumps and when you are feeling the touch of the Spirit, when you are feeling the nearness of the Holy Spirit, it means God wants to reveal some things to you. Those experiences mean God wants to communicate some things to you.

As the lady who wrote the letter to me was listening to my teaching, she was receiving information because she was already prepared. If you are a scientist or a researcher who is privileged to have this book in your hands right now, you could direct your mind to your area of activities. You can shift your mind to your area of practice and you could begin to meditate on ideas. You can connect that anointing you are feeling and that presence of God you are feeling right back to your profession, right back to your laboratory, right back to your research or whatever you are working on. When you begin to engage the Spirit of God, you will begin to make much more progress in understanding. You will begin to understand things better. You will begin to see things that are not clear before, you will begin to see with clarity, God will begin to lead you. You will no longer grope in darkness. You are going to see more clearly. You are going to feel some sharpness. You are going to see some laser focus coming to you and you will begin to download.

That is however only possible when your mind is prepared, that can only happen when your mind has been developed to be able to receive some very particular information. Your mind must be able to process.

CONVERT THROUGH A DEVELOPED MIND

The problem with many Christians and believers is that they go to worship God with a developed spirit but not with enough developed mind. They go to worship God, they feel the anointing of God, they feel the presence of God, and they feel the inspiration of the Holy Spirit but with a poor mind frame. They are not able to interpret what they get. They are not able to convert their experiences. Conversion is impossible without understanding, and for you to have understanding you must have a developed mind.

So you must have been researching something. You must have been working on something, then when the spirit of God comes He leads you right into it. God's spirit leads you into the projection of whatever you have been working on. There is no way the anointing of God is going to benefit you if you have not developed your mind. If you do not know anything, then you do not understand anything. If you have not been working on anything at all, you will only have the feeling and the goosebumps. Your only thought will be the goosebumps that the anointing brings.

There are many people who are just feeling the touch of God but do not know what to do with it. Are you also just feeling the inspiration but do not know what to do with it? It is absolutely counter-productive to be religious or to be striving to know God or to get closer to God, without developing yourself in any particular area or without pursuing your goal. Without self-development, without constant growth, and without cultivating your ground, your activities are futile and your promised land will lie fallow.

HOW TO HAVE A DEVELOPED MIND

In order to have a developed mind you need to work on cultivating yourself. The number one place to cultivate is your mind. It is a sign of responsibility that you are cultivating yourself. You start the cultivation by adding value to yourself, by developing yourself, by educating yourself, and by becoming an expert in your area of calling and becoming an expert in your promised land.

When you are good and you are an expert, entering into the presence of God will always begin the leading of God for you. You will know exactly what to convert whatever you have been studying into. You will know what to convert into whatever you are doing or engaged in. When you already have a developed mind, you are already skillful in one thing or the other. It is only then you will know exactly what the wave of the Spirit and the inspiration of the Spirit is leading you into developing. You will know exactly what particular product that you must produce as the inspiration of God is coming. You will be able to have the understanding of the product. You will be able to have the understanding of the next step to take and the understanding of the right actions to take.

If there were certain things not clear to you before and things not comprehensible, they begin to become clear and comprehensible to you. When you begin to feel that sensation, when you begin to feel that inspiration, it will lead you right into understanding of what to do and how to do it right. That is the same thing we are supposed to be experiencing when we read the bible. That is the exact thing we are supposed to experience when we worship the Lord. Our spiritual experiences are supposed to lead us into production, into more productivity, into producing the best goods and services and valuables for the world. Our experiences are supposed to help us in adding values to the world. That is how you convert.

You convert through a prepared mind and through work. Work is one of the greatest tools of conversion, this is discussed in greater detail in a later chapter. Apart from work, the greatest and the most important tools of conversion is through the mind. Understanding is one of the greatest tools of conversion.

So this dear lady I mentioned earlier wrote to me and explained how well skilled she is in her job and in her profession. Despite her skillfulness, she did not have the inspiration. This woman did not know what to move or how to move. However, as she was listening to me, ideas began to flow to her and through her. She said she began scribbling down many films, many productions and many scripts to produce. She told me she was no more satisfied being a local champion. She said as she was listening to me, she was being inspired to be a world champion. "I want to take the world of movie industry, I want to impact my world, and I want to change my nation. I want to bring another level of productivity to my industry" she wrote.

That is how we take the kingdom of God to the world. That is how we subdue the world with the kingdom of God through the anointing of the Holy Spirit and developed mind. That is what Daniel did.

HOW TO IMPOSE GOD'S KINGDOM ON THE WORLD

Daniel had the anointing of the Holy Spirit but he still needed to develop his mind. When Daniel got to the university in Babylon, he disciplined himself to study. Because he already had the anointing of the Holy Spirit, he became wiser ten times more than all other students who were studying with him. With such a mind, he was able to bring together the knowledge of Babylon, the knowledge of the God of Israel and the anointing of the Holy Spirit. He was able to intensify his mind, he succeeded in activating his mind; he was able to produce a product. The result was visible and tangible, his presence was felt. He became the governor, and all his friends became governors in the land. They became rulers, they became in charge.

Christians are not taking charge of nations. Christians are not taking over the political realm, economic realm, technological realm, media realm, and every other sphere of life and influence. The reason is simple and can only be due to one thing. We either don't know what to do with the anointing we have got or we don't know what to do with our spiritual experiences. We often don't know how to convert our revelations, ideas and thoughts or we have not developed our mind.

In our given sphere of influence, we have not become the best. Many Christians have not become competitive enough such that even when we feel the anointing, we don't know how to convert it. Our mind is not developed enough to convert the things we feel and hear into some form of product. That is what I want to change as a Christian and that is what I want to see changed as a preacher. I want to change it because if Christians could understand this, there will be no Bill Gates competing with us. If we Christians could understand this, there is no way Steve Jobs will be overriding us. No unbeliever on earth will be able to compete with Christians.

When we come into this understanding, we will be the head everywhere. We will be the leader everywhere. We will be Daniels of this age, we will be Jacobs of this age, we will become Josephs of this age, we will become Davids of this age because we will be converting so fast.

Every time we read the Bible, it will be bringing the inspiration of God and the Spirit of God will be quickening some scriptures to us. Through the scriptures we read, we will always get ideas, creativity will come so fast and so easy. We will constantly get ideas of products, of services, of values to produce. Ideas will be coming to us to reform the music industry, of how to change the media, advancing the technological age, reforming the information industry, refining the communication industry. There will be so much ideas on how to build companies, improving commerce, rehabilitating the finance industry and banking.

Ideas should come each time we read the bible. When you read the bible every day or every week (it doesn't matter how often you read the bible). When you fail to convert what you read, it is all irrelevant and an activity in futility. The reason why you read the bible is that the word must become flesh. The bible that you are reading is supposed to be generating new ideas in you. It is supposed to be generating and giving birth to new ideas, new technology, new concept that the whole world has never thought about or heard before. When there is the combination of the inspiration of God and developed mind, the extraordinary is birthed and born.

Therefore, it is a disgrace when we claim to be Christians who know God, and there is nothing to show for it. It is a shame when we say we are interacting with God and we don't have anything to show for it. When we say we are having spiritual experiences and we do not have anything to show for it, we put God in dishonor.

WHAT MUST BE THE END-POINT OF SPIRITUAL EXPERIENCES?

What then must be the end point of spiritual experiences? Every spiritual experience we are having is supposed to produce some goods, some services, and some products. It is a disgrace that we say we are communicating with God and cannot speak before men.

In other words, it is disgraceful when God cannot speak to us on how to solve our economic problems. Is it that God cannot speak to us how to resolve our political issues, or the hunger problem of our nations? Can't anyone hear God on how to solve the problem of militancy or the menace of extreme poverty in our communities? It looks like God is not speaking, it looks like God is deaf, and dumb. It is not that God is deaf and dumb, it is because we are deaf and dumb. We have not developed our mind, we have not risen up in our understanding. We have not walked in the knowledge and understanding that Daniel walked in. We are yet to have and to walk in the knowledge and understanding that Moses walked in and that of Joseph in Egypt. We have limited ourselves to the four walls of the church just reading the bible and telling tales by moonlight.

The bible cannot profit you a thing if you cannot convert it. When you fail to convert, then everything is utterly useless. It is just spiritual emotions. You will only get emotions when your mind is not opened up and that will be all.

Apart from emotions, what are you producing? If you are reading the Bible, I want to see what you have produced as a result of that Bible. If you are praying or you claim to be a prayerful person, I want to see the results you have produced as a result of that prayer. If you go to church, I want to see the product that you have as a result of going to that church.

If you cannot show the world the product you have, if you cannot show me the evidence of your lifestyle, then you are totally irrelevant here on earth. Everything spiritual remains irrelevant until it is converted. If your spiritual experiences cannot be converted, they remain irrelevant. Only physical things, only tangible things are relevant on this side of the planet.

WHAT ARE THE THINGS THAT MUST BE CONVERTED?

Let me give you some points and instructions on those things that you need to begin to convert.

The first I will discuss is prayer. Our prayers must result in tangible results. Praying and meditation must become tangible products. How does that happen? When you pray, the main goal in prayers should be how you can be in relationship with the father. The main purpose of prayers is not to get bread and butter nor is it to get your needs met. The goal of praying is not to get what to eat, drink or wear. Rather, the main purpose in prayer is to acknowledge and to seek to be in contact with the father.

The next thing you want to do is to find out what the Father is thinking and what the desire of is heart is. You want to discover that which is in the mind of the Father. You want to download some information from the mind of the Father because the son cannot do anything except those things He sees the Father do. Your goal in prayers is to understand what God is doing. It is to understand what is it that God wants to do in your nation and in your sphere of influence.

You want to find out what are the wisdom God will apply if He were to be in your position and in your situation. It is to understand what God is thinking concerning your situation, to understand what He would have done differently, what He would have done in your place. These are the things your mind should focus on when you pray every day.

Prayer should not be monotonous and boring. When you are praying, you are not just doing a one-way direction activity, rather you are trying to see in the Spirit. When you pray, you are trying to feel that anointing, that inspiration that gives you the idea. In prayer, you are thinking about your sphere of influence and talking to God. It is then the anointing is coming upon you, you are directing your thought right into that thing you are thinking about or you are wondering about. You are releasing your mind into the hand of God and the inspiration of God will come to you. This inspiration will quicken your mind. It will quicken your spirit and you will be able to remember things and get some ideas about what you are working on. That is how you see the Father. That is how to pray.

Then, when you see what the Father is doing, the next thing you are supposed to do is to leave the place of prayer and turn right out there. You must go now and begin to work hard. You must begin to implement and to convert what you have seen and heard.

Whatsoever you have seen in the spirit must become real tangible substances through mental work. This has to be done in order to convert what you have seen in the spirit into the language of men.

That is how prayer is converted into product. Do you remember the lady I talked about earlier who wrote a letter to me? The same thing happened in her story.

She was listening to me. While she was doing that, a conversion was happening inside her and she began writing down those things. Then she wrote me her letter as well.

She also wrote of other times when together with her friends she had long sessions of prayer. When they were praying, some people were prophesying (they were seeing what was happening in the Spirit) but she did not know what to do with it. She was only hearing the prophecy but could not understand nor make meaning of it.

Later on, she heard me preach about conversion, she then remembered those prophecies that were given concerning her. Now she has begun to convert the prophecies into ideas and she began to write them down. Through hard work, she is going to convert the ideas into tangible products.

This dear lady explained lastly in her letter another experience as well. She has the grace and ability of leading people into song worship alongside her other gifts and grace.

She said after listening to me teach on conversion and each time she worships, she begins to feel the inspiration of the Holy Spirit. When she begins to feel the inspiration of the Holy Spirit she releases her mind and allows the Spirit of God to hover her mind. Whenever she does this, she notices that incubation is happening right away.

The goose bumps are due to the inspiration of the Holy Spirit. During the incubation of the Holy Spirit, you release your mind you think on whatever project is going on, you begin to think about whatever it is you are producing. The inspiration of the almighty God, the hovering of his Spirit and the inspiration of the Spirit quickens your mind. You will know exactly the idea and what you suppose to do. You should then quickly put those things you got down. Now is the time to get the formula together, put your things together, the idea and information you have got. Now, immediately leave the place of prayer, go and begin to do the research. Begin to work physically into the realization of the things you have received in the Spirit.

That is how you convert praise and worship experience into products. That is how you convert as well your prayer experience into valuable product. That is what our spiritual life is supposed to be about. Spiritual experiences must not just be noise making from morning till night without anything to show for it. When we engage in wild dancing, lots of noise and lifting of hands without tangible products to show after everything, it is mere religion. Such a life is not Christianity, it is religion and religion is a monster. I'm sure you remember such a life was the life of the prophets of Baal on Mount Carmel.

Let me prove this to you again. In Luke 4, Jesus Christ was taken to the mountain. In the very first verse, He went into the mountain to pray and fast for forty days. If Jesus had only gone to the mountain to pray and nothing happened after all, that is, if there was no conversion, then that meant the fasting was irrelevant.

He needed to convert that which he went to pray about. Whatever he prayed about must be converted.

Immediately in same chapter, we saw Jesus converting His experience on the mountain into a concrete conversion. What did He convert it to? In verse fourteen the bible says He came back in the power of the Holy Spirit. That power was God given. It was not His own conversion, it was what happened through God. He invested Himself in the Spirit and God imparted Him with power.

Now that power had to be converted into real physical energy, it had to become physical product for it to bring relevance to humanity. When Jesus was on the mountain, He released His mind to God and God gave Him ideas. He knew exactly the concept and idea of what He ought to do. So when He came back from the mountain after forty days, He had already the knowledge and steps of what to do. He went into the temple and picked the book of the law, the book of prophet Isaiah about His life, and this is what He read:

"The Spirit of the Lord is on me, because he has anointed me to proclaim good news to the poor. He has sent me to proclaim freedom for the prisoners and recovery of sight for the blind, to set the oppressed free, to proclaim the year of the Lord's favor." (vs. 18-19)(NIV)

The Spirit is something invisible, it is something spiritual. From his experiences, Jesus also went to the mountain. There, He got anointed. Anointing also is invisible as well as spirit is invisible. Jesus converted through preaching and worked the anointing. He converted the Spirit upon Him to becoming a blessing to the poor, healing to the broken hearted, visible life changes to other human beings, liberation to the poor, deliverance for the captives. He converted his spirit into opening of eye sight to the blind, into liberty to those who were bruised and into acceptable year of the Lord to the whole world.

Now you see dear friend, Jesus' anointing and His power of the Holy Spirit were meant to bring concrete, tangible blessings, to the life of humanity and to individual lives. His anointing was to be converted into blessings for physical body, flesh and blood. Anointing was to be converted into somebody's healed body. Anointing was to be converted into food that will feed five thousand. Anointing was to be converted into opening of prison yard for people who have been in bondage. The invisible revelations, experiences in themselves had no meaning until they became blessing unto other people.

The invisible blessings must and are going to be converted into visible, tangible blessings to real physical human beings. It is the same thing that is supposed to happen today. The similarity is this; in those days, the anointing of Jesus was not just converted to bring about spiritual blessings. It was converted to bring about tangible and physical blessings as well.

Through laboratory, library, research development and advancement, through whatever will make the earth look like heaven, through strategies and ideas that will make His kingdom come on earth as it is in heaven. We must become preoccupied with the desire to make the kingdom of this world become a look alike of heaven. We must become obsessed with anything that will make the earth to look like heaven. Those are the ideas God will give you. He is going to give you inspirations that will make life on this earth to be more tolerable, more adaptable. God is going to give you the plan, design and scheme that will make the earth become a replica of heaven. That is what the blessings of God is meant for.

HOW TO CONVERT WORDS OF PROPHECY INTO TANGIBLE PRODUCTS

Our words of prophecy which are given by God must be converted to tangible products. When our words of prophecy are not converted into tangible results, they remain irrelevant and ineffectual. Such prophecies that are not converted will not profit anyone. So every word of prophecy, just like the word of God that was with God in the beginning became flesh must be converted to become flesh.

Luke 2:25-27 states

"Now there was a man in Jerusalem called Simeon, who was righteous and devout. He was waiting for the consolation of Israel, and the Holy Spirit was on him. It had been revealed to him by the Holy Spirit that he would not die before he had seen the Lord's Messiah. Moved by the Spirit, he went into the temple courts. When the parents brought in the child Jesus to do for him what the custom of the Law required"

Furthermore, Luke 4: 25-27 also reported that *"it was revealed unto him i.e. Simeon, the coming of the Messiah. Simeon had prophesied about the coming of the Lord Jesus Christ and God has promised him that he will not die until Jesus was given birth to."*

The promise, prophecy and the fulfillment came to pass. He did not die until he saw Jesus Christ. It was after seeing Jesus that he died and went to heaven. This means the prophecy was materialized. He saw Jesus Christ, the prophesied Messiah physically before he left this world.

So your own prophecy must also be converted unto realization and physical manifestation, otherwise it will become irrelevant. Our words of prophecy must be converted into tangible physical results or else the prophecies will only become mere entertainment.

To a large extent prophecies among some Christian circles has been reduced to mere entertainment that we use to console each other. We often console each other with words of prophecies that we don't know when and if they will come to pass. But when it is the real manifestation of God, prophecies come to pass. People who know God always see prophecies come to pass.

It is not only of itself that prophecies come to pass, sometimes you need to carry out certain responsibilities. In fact, every word of prophecy has a component of responsibility to be carried out before it can come to fulfillment.

The bible says Simeon was there physically. He could not bring the child forth physically, but he saw the child after he was born. Now, when they brought Jesus Christ into the temple, the Spirit of God came upon Simeon and moved him to go into the temple. He saw the messiah (this refers to the physical manifestation). He saw the physical conversion of his own prophecy. That is why the bible says *"let your light so shine before the world that they will see."* Your light that is shining are all the spiritual blessings that you have.

So let your blessings, your spiritual experiences, your grace, your anointing shine before the world. When you do this, they (the people of the world) will see.

Your light has to be taken into the world, it has to be taken to the people in the darkness. It is only when your light shines among the people in the darkness that they will see. It is when they see that they will glorify your Father who is in heaven. If they cannot see, they cannot glorify God.

People can only see something that is tangible. People can only see something that is expressible, some products, some substance. So, what is the benefit of the prophecies that you have been receiving all these years? Have they been converted? It is just like the dear lady that I wrote about in the earlier parts of this chapter who was a dramatist and a worship leader, she said she had always received prophecies and many people had prophesied to her. In an instance, many women were prophesying to her for several hours. They were telling her about the movies that she is going to produce and how God was going to use her mightily in the movie industry. Even though the prophecies were coming, she did not know how to convert. She needed to go and convert those prophecies into tangible effects and manifestations.

A lot of people are receiving prophecies and waiting for God to convert it for them. There is a side of God which many people are yet to discover. That side of God reflects that though God has brought the blessings, the inspiration, and the information to you, you will have to do your own part by going to develop your mind.

Work with your mind and you will know what you need to do to bring every prophecy to pass. You need to convert through hard work. You need mental work, physical work, and spiritual work. You need to convert your prophecy to tangible manifestation.

THE SCRIPTURES WE READ MUST BE CONVERTED INTO PROOFS

Moreover, the scriptures that we read must be carried out into physical manifestations. Whenever we read the scripture, the question must be asked, "How can this word become flesh? What physical manifestation can I turn this to? What idea is God giving me?"

Whatever it is that we read both in the old and New Testament is full of invention. In fact the Bible is a book of inventions. From the beginning to the end, we can discover the mind of God and what he wants to bring about on the earth.

As we read our bible, we must allow the Holy Spirit to minister to us, but we must have a developed mind first. If you don't have a developed mind, reading the scriptures will be a mere routine. You will keep seeing and saying what everybody is seeing and saying. You will not be able to see anything unique. If your mind is developed in any area, though you are not a preacher you will be able to connect some truths of the scriptures, some inspiration of the Spirit, to your area of specialization.

You will begin to see in the scriptures certain interpretations and deep meanings into what you are doing. You will be able to produce new products, new services, and new values. If you know how to read the bible with the anointing and you have developed your mind, there will be some conversions taking place each time you read the scriptures.

For example, Jesus proclaimed that he was called to preach good news to the poor. What is good news to the poor?

Now, I want to convert the anointing upon me to good news to the poor in Nigeria, in Africa because my country and my continent is poor. The very first thing that the anointing upon Jesus Christ is supposed to do is to deliver good news to the poor. It means that the anointing must be converted into some form of good news to the impoverished. It means that if the anointing is truly upon me, it must bring the poor out of their poverty so that they will not see themselves as poor anymore. That anointing must be able to convert to them what they need. The anointing must wipe off the tears of widows and orphans so that they will not need to cry any longer before they go to bed. It must be able to convert to them the food they need so that they will not live everyday hungry. It must be able to convert for them the resources, the finances that they need to be able to provide for themselves. The anointing must send poor children to school and cause them to be able to aspire in life. The anointing must make the jobless get decent jobs, make decent money, so that they will not live a miserable life anymore. That is what the anointing does.

When I read the scriptures, I am not just reciting it. That is what many pastors do today, repeating the stories that everybody in the kindergarten Sunday school know already. They are not telling us how to convert the stories into real life manifestations.

The way to convert the story is to tell the people that everything is possible for them. People have to convert the stories into zeal, passion, and goals. Let people know that if they can be result oriented, passionate, goal focused, and if they live for and by results, they will be able to get to any height. They will be able to get God's power and anointing and create everything they need.

People's goals can be met, their dreams can come true, people can subdue any mountain. Every impossibility in their lives can be resolved.

For example, if you lack electricity in your country, it is not anything new. It is in the Bible as well. God himself had to deal with the problem of darkness and declared light into existence. The possibility of bringing electricity to your country is achievable. If you have goals and you live for that goal, shunning every other thing, you can succeed in bringing electricity to your own country. You can eliminate poverty in your environment if you choose to so focus on that. You will be able to achieve any goal if you can dedicate yourself to that goal, you can live for that goal and lock yourself into that goal.

This is how the stories we read in the scriptures are supposed to be converted into physical manifestations in everyone's life. When people see the solutions you have brought, they will rejoice at your birth and existence. They will choose to worship and glorify your God. If you are reading this right now, you must decide not to just read the same stories of the bible written two thousand years ago as mere letters. We are trying to tell people that God is powerful.

We say to people that God can heal the issue of blood, that he cures leprosy and even raised the dead. The question however is this "what can we do as people created in God's image?"

The reason why God is showing us what He can do is to show us what we can do. The life of Jesus is our master example. If Jesus fed the poor, we should also find out in our understanding how we can build food industries that will be able to feed people. If Jesus used His grace and anointing to resolve things that are impossible, we should be looking for things that seem impossible in this world to resolve. Current examples include healing for cancer, sugar diabetes and numerous other incurable diseases bringing many nations to their knees. That is an example for us. We must choose to use the inspirations of Jesus; the healings that Jesus did must be converted into the healing of sugar diabetes, healing of HIV AIDS, healing of cancer. This is the reason we should read our bible. The purpose of reading and studying must not just be for repeating the same stories all over. We are to read our bibles in order to convert what is in our bibles into real physical manifestation.

The bible says in Luke 4 verse 21

"He (Jesus) began by saying to them, today this scripture is fulfilled in your hearing."

Can you imagine that? Jesus was saying that the mere fact he was standing among them, that prophecy was going to be fulfilled. He will ensure that the words were converted and became their normal experience. The purpose of the word is to be fulfilled, to become flesh. The word was with God in the beginning, but it remained irrelevant until it became flesh.

So if you are reading the bible every day, you must begin to ask yourself, "How can I convert this word into my area of passion, calling, profession, and economy? How can these words become the usual experience for people of my country? How can everyone around me benefit and how can the people of my country begin to have experiences similar to this? You must not just read the bible religiously. Religion profits nothing. Religion profits no one, it only creates nuisance of people.

The letters of the scriptures, the letters of the book profit nothing. It is only the Spirit's anointing with your developed mentality that can be of benefit to people.

When developed with some research and information and you go to work like that on the idea, you convert that impression into physical manifestations. That is when reading the word of God becomes beneficial. It didn't just stop in the area of feelings, goose bumps and emotions but it produced something tangible as it was in the case of Jesus. That was how we got saved. We beheld His glory and He became a salvation tool to all of us.

IDEAS MUST BE CONVERTED INTO TANGIBLE PRODUCTS

Ideas that we get from God must also not be just ideas and mental impressions or feelings, they must be converted through mental work. You must convert every idea that comes to you into physical manifestation. You must make sure that ideas are manifested, converted, and implemented into the real world. They must become some visible tangible product through your effort, hard work, and physical work. People must be able to see the product of hard work in your life. Again, that is why the bible says let your light so shine before the men of the world. Men will see the product of your idea, and when they see that, they will glorify your father who is in heaven. Otherwise you are just engaging in religion. Otherwise you are just building a religious career. People who are full of religion are empty of God. Such people are not God-carriers, they are not living like Jesus.

Every word that God spoke got converted. When God said let there be light, we saw the light come forth. For everything in the spirit to become beneficial, they must become tangible (physical), every word must become flesh. It is only when your spiritual experiences become manifested physically that they become beneficial.

John 19 vs. 36 says that: *"These things were done, that the Scripture should be fulfilled, a bone of him shall not be broken."(NIV)*

At crucifixion, the bones of his body were actually not broken. This is physical manifestation. Your relevance is only to the material world, so don't try to escape the material world. Your reason of relating with the spiritual world is to bring your spiritual experiences into the material world. You can bring the spiritual into the physical through mental, physical work. Everything we see today comes from the invisible world.

Your love, visions, revelations must be converted to products. A lot of us are just stimulating and masturbating ourselves through the so-called revelations, preaching, messages without conversion into physical, tangible products. It is likened to spiritual masturbation because it brings momentary pleasure without conception, no seed, no fruit.

Again, that is why Matthew 26 vs. 56 says:

"But this has all taken place that the writings of the prophets might be fulfilled." Then all the disciples deserted him and fled."

It is all about fulfillment, all the disciples forsook Jesus because of prophecy. A lot of people are merely stimulating themselves with rhema, revelations, jumping, singing, dancing etc. Without conversion into physical tangible products, all rhemas and revelations are just self-stimulations.

Lastly, we read from the bible in John 13 verse 18: Here the Bible was saying

"I am not referring to all of you; I know those I have chosen. But this is to fulfill this passage of Scripture: 'He who shared my bread has turned against me."

It is all about fulfillment. Every action, every movement, every deed was to bring about the fulfillment of that which had been said or written. Every prophecy in the scriptures was fulfilled in the bible and we saw the physical manifestation of it. Many church folks have become out rightly spiritual and want to escape the material world. That is why we have become so irrelevant on the earth. Our dreams and visions are meant to be manifested physically to bless the human race and give glory to God.

John 17 vs. 12 declares *"While I was with them, I protected them and kept them safe by that name you gave me. None has been lost except the one doomed to destruction so that Scripture would be fulfilled."*

Another fulfillment of prophecy was confirmed here. Today we do a lot of spiritual activities and have nothing to show for it. When we begin to convert our spiritual experiences into tangible products, Christians will have many inventions, products, innovations, creations, designs, constructions, devices, gadgets, wonder machines and discoveries than we could ever imagine. Christians will be the ones in Forbes magazines, Christians will be found in Guinness book of world records declaring the majesty of the king, more Christians will be found on the list of Nobel

Prize winners. Christians will be the ones ruling this world claiming back the earth for God, imposing and blanketing the earth with the majesty of the King.

GOLDEN NUGGETS
FROM CHAPTER 4

- The most important word you will ever learn in your life is the word "conversion."

- You must understand that anything that God is giving you in the Spirit must become products.

- Conversion is impossible without understanding

- The number one place to cultivate is your mind.

- Ideas should come each time we read the bible.

- It is a disgrace that we say we are communicating with God and cannot speak before men.

- Our praying and meditation must become tangible products.

CHAPTER 5

HOW TO MAKE
TANGIBLE PRODUCTS
ON THE EARTH

At this time and age, Christians need to be taught all over again how to live on earth. Many have gone so far into heaven and into spiritual world and superstitious things that most Christians are no longer relevant on earth.

Statistics shows Christians are the least group amongst those contributing and producing on the earth. They are producing the least technological feats in the world. Christians are not among the best inventors, professors and producers of goods and services. Christians have been left behind.

Whereas if you look back into history, 600-700 years ago, Christians were ruling the world. Our civilization is a Christian civilization, thanks to European renaissance, and renaissance is the celebration of knowledge.

Before renaissance, the church controlled the key of knowledge. The church controlled every affair that people were involved in such as education, marriage, government etc. The Church made everything have the appearance of spirituality. They taught that we are only here temporarily, hence you do not need to go to school or read, similar to what many are doing today preparing for heaven and refusing to go to school. Women would not go to school, some went to school only to become priests. People went to school only to study something spiritual but what did that lead to?

It led to backwardness at such a level that Christians locked themselves so much in church. The language of Church became the language of school. Scientific education was taken away from people and things could only be learnt in Latin. At the time, you could not access knowledge unless you were learning to be a priest or learning Catholicism. The only profession was theology and catechism. There was no progress, no understanding and there was no light.

THE DARK AGES

The absence of light through the whole of the earth threw the entire age into total darkness. Those moments became the dark ages.

Dark ages, so much in the sense that horrible things happened at the time. Those schooling to be priests were committing atrocities yet the only things people did was become priests. People went to monasteries and convents and perpetuated severe atrocities. Nuns were getting pregnant and people were killed who opposed religion.

If you dared by accident try to preach the gospel not prescribed by state or read the Bible for yourself, you were put in Prison. You could not preach or talk about the Holy

Spirit , if you did you stood the risk of being burnt at the stake or being burnt by fire.

If you argued with the Church, horrible things were done to you. This period was historic and the time of inquisition began. Inquisition was an historic period when no one dared to question the doctrines of the church.

It was also the era of 'The Crusade' when entire people of other religions were killed and wiped out by Christians. The Church excommunicated and killed many inventors and scientists like Galileo Galilei. Examples of others who were severely persecuted were:

Michael Servetus (who first described blood circulation between the heart and lungs). He was burnt alive by the church.

Hypatia (renowned historian who was killed by a Christian mob, driven into a rage by claims that she was interfering in a religious dispute between the Governor and the Bishop of Alexandria)

Antoine Lavoisier(who first wrote the first list of the chemical elements — a forerunner of the periodic table and further found that about 20 percent of air is oxygen and that when something burns, it is actually reacting chemically with oxygen. Lavoisier's theory of combustion debunked the then popular theory of 'phlogiston.') His head was chopped off by the Church.

Giordano Bruno (the view that the earth orbits the sun, and that the earth is not the center of the universe. More than this, he held the thoroughly modern view that distant stars are orbited by their own, possibly inhabited, planets. He stated that the universe is infinite in size and has no center). For his view, the Church burnt him alive also.

I can cite many more examples of how the Church fought civilization by their religious views. Religion in any form is extremely dangerous. Many intelligent and brilliant minds were severely persecuted, killed and all their research, works and publications completely burned.

Anytime an authority, for example religious authority tries to silence the people, it always leads to backwardness and dark ages. The theory of the time led to inquisition, and because you could not question anything, the church made away with anything they wanted. That led to Crusades which Christians started, wars to take back the holy land which has led to hatred of Christians till today by the Muslims in the Middle East.

What I am saying is that any attempt to keep everything in the church and to keep knowledge from people will always lead to atrocities and dark ages. Our attempt to remain just in the spirit will always be counterproductive. The attempt to keep people to reading just spiritual books is leading them back to the Dark Age. Churches are limiting a lot of people to just becoming Pastors and engaging in only spiritual activities. That will lead to the degradation of humanity. People will begin to witch hunt in Church with Church members attacking and abusing one another. People will begin attacking each other for having an opinion and everyone will begin rebelling against authority. Our attempt to try to be spiritual is religion and these are the results.

WE MUST EXPLORE THE PHYSICAL

God made us material and physical and we must learn to function in the physical world. Our goal is not to escape the physical and the material world instead our goal is to be comfortable here and to agree with the fact that God made us physical beings. It was not Satan who made us physical beings, it was God who made us material beings and he wants us to operate and explore this material world. God does not make us experience the spirit realm just for exploration, when you explore the spirit realm it is to be beneficial on the earth.

If you are not converting all of your spirituality into material benefit, it is a waste of time. The whole goal of God causing us to be here on earth is for it to be manifested in physical and material form.

Remember, God created the earth as a prototype of heaven but heaven is already spiritual. If he wanted another spiritual entity, he would have made the earth as such. He would not have created us as physical beings. The reason God made us in the physical and material was because that was what he needed. He needed us to be physical and function as such. If that was not needed then we wouldn't have been created as such.

Why am I saying this? For you Christians who are so super-spiritual, I want to bring you down a little bit to your relevance here. If God needed you in heaven now he would kill you and take you to himself immediately, But since you are still existing in the material world, it is because you are needed in the material world.

If you don't do this, you will never be able to fulfill God's calling upon yourself. If you try to be spiritual alone, it will always be counterproductive. The last time this was ignored, there was widespread atrocity. When you try to escape you are conflicting with God's plan. When you try to escape the physical reality of your life, you are fighting against God and you are swimming against the tide. When you do that you are trying to communicate to God that you do not belong here and that God made a mistake. Do you think God does not know what he is doing? Your very attempt to try to be spiritual must only be for the benefit of the earth.

THE PURPOSE OF FELLOWSHIP

We all need to fellowship and our spirit must always be in tune with God. At the end of the day, the reason our spirit needs fellowship with God is to be able to understand what God wants to do on the earth. What is his will and what are his desires on the earth? By interacting with Him we discover His mind and His intention and then we bring and transmit these intentions from heaven to the earth. That is the only reason we fellowship in the spirit and interact with the Holy Spirit.

We seek to understand the reality of the spirit in heaven and to transfer that reality to the earth. The reality of God wiping away the tears of the people and the reality of living a sickness free life and the reality of building streets of gold and anything that is present in the kingdom of God and to transmit those realities to the earth. That way we fulfill the desire and the mandate of God to us which is thy kingdom come on earth as it is in heaven…whatever is in heaven and is obtainable in heaven must come to the earth.

We need these experiences to see what is obtainable in heaven. We need those experiences to know what is obtainable in heaven and to be able to convert those realities to earth. This is why we say thy kingdom come, thy will be done on earth as it is in heaven. The goal is not heaven, the goal is earth. Whatever is in heaven must come. The things in heaven that we try to escape into must be transferred to this earth. This is what life is about on the earth. When we talk about life on the earth, we only have this once in a lifetime chance to bring these things to the earth. This is why we fellowship with God.

This is the experience in the Garden of Eden, God fellowshipped and interacted with man. They saw what was obtainable in God's kingdom and they began to implement it on the earth. They implemented that on the earth by naming animals, taking care of herbs, cultivating fruits and so on. They got their instructions and didn't just remain there, they applied whatever they got on the earth. Whatever they got was supposed to be used on the earth because the goal of God for the earth is for the earth to be a duplicate of heaven.

You must make an attempt to pay careful attention to this instruction.

YOUR CALLING SHOULD PRODUCE FRUIT

Only tangible things benefit people on earth. The earth is meant for only physical tangible things. Where are your tangible fruits, product and results? I'm not talking about giving birth to children, I'm talking about whatever you created.

The reason why this message is so important is because many think they are not to become ambitious and anyone talented is immediately ordained a Pastor. That is horrible. Anyone doing anything good immediately becomes a 5 fold minister. That is also horrible.

I have a book that will give you more insight into callings, the book is titled 'Who Am I'. Many think callings are only spiritual, not many know they are called to be scientists, cooks and so on. Many do not know they are called to resolve social problems or to be politicians or be information technologists. We look at those things as if they are only professions. We often don't know that spiritual callings are only about 1-2%. 99% of us are supposed to have calling to the earth.

Our calling is supposed to be in the world with real tangible results. We are supposed to create tangible, physical results. People who are called to fix roads have already gone to preach or to become Bible school teachers. People who are supposed to fix economy are on Prayer Mountains. These things are counterproductive.

We are going to lack God's kingdom on earth that way and we end up fighting each other. Instead for them to be more productive, people become counterproductive.

If you put too much light into the room where you are now it will blind every eye and we won't be able see any longer. Same way, too much light in the church is not good. Light is not meant for the church alone. The light that is in church must be sent to the world. We create problems when we concentrate all the light in the church and there is a lot of infighting.

We are supposed to know that we can serve God with our gifts and talents, our hands, minds and legs. We should know that we can have a calling and we can produce something tangible for the world. We are supposed to be producing something tangible. We are supposed to be bringing forth something that will make the world better and will make the world have resemblance to heaven. We must begin to see the pictures of things in heaven and begin to reproduce them on the earth.

THE GOAL IS HEAVEN ON EARTH

What is the proof of this that I'm talking about?

If you are trying to be spiritual and sticking to just fasting and praying, something is missing. Of course, we should fast and pray. I do that but we must engage fasting just like Jesus did. We must discover what God is doing in heaven and bring it to the earth. We ought to see the result of your prayer and fasting.

We don't just want to know that you have been in church for donkey years, what is the result? Without fruit, church going becomes a waste of time. We want to see the result of what you have done or achieved.

In my book 'Only God can save Nigeria –What a Myth', I have made a similar claim.

Some people think that for them to serve God they need to be in Church all the time, praying, fasting and doing a lot of other things which are true, but the purpose of praying and fasting is conversion.

When Moses went to pray and fast, he came back with something tangible after forty days. He did not just come back prophesying, he came back with proof and results and products. He came back with the Ten Commandments. He converted what he saw on the mountain to something physical. God showed him what He wanted him to do. God wanted him to bring out the Ten Commandments and he did. Our spiritual experience should deliver something concrete and tangible to us in the physical realm.

ONLY TANGIBLE THINGS BENEFIT PEOPLE ON EARTH

Let's talk about Noah, he also went to the mountain to spend time with God and came back with definite instructions. He came back with strategies, sketches on how to build the ark. His spiritual experience when he went to pray and fast was converted into something physical and he created the ark from a result of his encounter with God. I don't really respect people who say they have been Christians for years without anything tangible that their life and Christianity has produced. If your Christian experience is not producing tangible things in the world, you are only giving birth to religion. The way things work on the earth is that spiritual experiences must be converted into something tangible on the earth for it to benefit man.

When Moses did forty days of fasting and praying, he came back with a clear understanding of building the tabernacle from his encounter with God. That is how our life is supposed to be.

What has your going to church given birth to? What have you constructed, created or produced. What are the things we can point to that your going to church has created? If people like Steve Jobs are just doing their own meditation and have ideas to improve our world and make our world like heaven, what are Christians catching and creating? Do you think God just has spiritual revelations but he lacks ideas on how to create cars, jets, telecommunications, does He lack ideas for computers?

Is He only good for calling out your bank account numbers, your telephone numbers, healing? Does He not understand the world, can't He help us? He can! We only need to be ready.

Of course, if He could give ideas to Noah for constructing an ark that preserved the world, don't tell me that God is dead or has disappeared. He cannot be a one time show God. He still gives ideas that supersedes the titanic even the Boeing engine. Yes, he does but we are not studying. We just want to remain in the spirit yet we are not converting. If you have to convert then your mind must be developed. We are not developing our minds enough to compete with the people of the world. Even if you are the only human on earth that is the closest to God, if your mind is not developed enough, God cannot give you an idea of submarines. This is simply because you won't know what submarines are.

You cannot say the same God who gave the idea for the wonderful tabernacle when there were no excavators, computers and so on is no more capable. God gave a very detailed description such that they were able to build a superb tabernacle. You can't say He is no more capable and only good for giving prophecies that never come to pass. Prophecies of suffering, death, money and seed sowing. Is that the only thing He is capable of doing? What do we really think of our God? What have we made God to look like to the inhabitants of the earth? The same God that gave ideas to Joseph, or you think all Joseph did was prophesy?

TANGIBLE PRODUCTS ARE
CREATED BY CONVERSION

Joseph was a prophet but did not just prophesy, he went beyond that to interpret how things are supposed to be born in the physical world. The whole value of the gift was that he was able to convert the spiritual experiences into material realities. He was able to convert the revelations into tangible products.

Whatever is not converted; preaching, anointing, spiritual exercises etc when not converted into tangible expressional forms are totally irrelevant. In fact, it is the conversion that made Joseph who he was. It was the conversion that made him a supernatural human being on the earth. Ideas must be converted. Anyone who became great on the earth did because they converted ideas.

We talk of Steve Jobs and Bill Gates because they converted the ideas that they had.

They converted the ideas they have and we are supposed to have access to more ideas, revelations and encounters with God in the spirit. What are you converting it to? What are your results?

Joseph converted his, Noah converted his, Moses converted his, what are you converting?

What Joseph converted catapulted him into greatness.

He himself was a man of revelation and a prophet. As a prophet, God was able to entrust him with ideas. He had such a close relationship with God that God could show him how to build storage systems. The Math, physics, chemicals, and all that needed to be done to conserve food for 14 years and large storage to feed the entire world. He was able to conceive that in his mind and he was able to supersede the realities on earth.

From that idea, the Egyptians got the idea of pyramids. These things are there in the spirit. Many things are there in the spirit. As long as it is in the spirit, it is not benefiting us. The only way it can benefit us is if we convert everything that we see in the spirit. When we convert all that we see, then it can benefit the earth and mankind. Joseph converted everything that he saw.

Same thing happened with Daniel because he was able to convert the revelation and dream of the king into understandable matter. He was able to convert that into real life communication. I don't care how spiritual you are and I don't care how religious, what I care about is what you have converted your spiritual experiences into.

Even God himself would have remained irrelevant on the earth if not for conversion. In the book of Genesis, before Genesis there was God, yet the Bible says in Gen. 1: 1, that God in the beginning created the heaven and the earth. Why does he need to do that? Why did He need to create something tangible and visible from the invisible realm? He was all sufficient and all satisfactory. He was there from millions of years and billions of years. Yet, when He wanted to bring relevance to the earth and recognition to man, He had to do something physical. He could only manifest himself through some physical material way. God in his spirit form had to come to earth to manifest and materialize.

He had to come to earth to produce something physical, tangible and visible. He had to create a visible tangible earth. Then he could create us from that and when he created us we could talk about God. God would have been irrelevant if he never created something tangible.

The one who is truly spiritual is God, His spirituality is no joke yet despite his spirituality he had to reduce himself into physical manifestation. He had to leave and abandon the spirituality and convert himself into tangibility. That is how he created the earth to function. He created the earth for tangible manifestation. If he converted his spirituality and you are trying to escape the tangible and physical world and realities, then you are doing the world and yourself disservice. Your relevance can only be material. Even God with all his spiritual reality had to prove himself in tangibility.

That is why Churches should stop turning people to fools like churches did in the dark ages.

If something is not done quickly, I see the dark ages coming back to the Church. The dark ages in the sense that churches just keep people idly in a place begging and hoping to go to heaven, many times these people cannot pursue the mandate of God upon their individual lives.

In Nigeria for example, out of a population of about 180 million people, statistics says that about 61.2 % of these people are Christians which is about 100 million people in total. Let's even assume that only 50 million people go to Church, the question is, what are these 50 million people doing? How can you have 50 million believers in a country and the country is as it is today?

Churches should not reduce people to morons. Atheists were birthed in dark ages when their thinking was taken. We are repeating same mistake and hardening the heart of intellectuals. If we are not careful, our children and grand-children may not come to church because we have made the church seem so backward and irrelevant. We have made everything seem so spiritual and everyone thinks we have lost our minds. If God who is truly spiritual had to re-duce himself to making physical things, what do we think of ourselves. Are you going to be more holy and spiritual than God? After your forty and fifty days fast, please bring the proof. Let's see, let the unbelievers see. Prove it by con-version. Let's see what the fast has done to you.

RESULTS PROVE THE AUTHENTICITY OF YOUR EXPERIENCE

After you have visited all the mountains, show us the result.

It is result we are interested in, if you cannot show the result, I don't care if you were there for a hundred years. That was what Jesus was telling the disciples after having spiritual experiences on the mountain and yet could not deliver an epileptic man.

Jesus was frustrated at them because they only wanted to experience spirituality. We are separating spirituality from physical realm and realities, he told them to bring the child to him. If I have been to the mountain then my depth and spirituality must be demonstrated in real life. He commanded the demon out and made the young man healthy. He converted the anointing into health. He converted the anointing into feeding people. He was always converting his spiritual experiences with God into physical manifestations. What is your own spirituality changing?

What is changing in your country, economy and in your society? What is it contributing to humanity?

I have been able to convert my anointing into impact here in Ukraine. Wait till I get to Africa, the results in Ukraine will be a child's play. When we understand this truth, the Church in Africa can transform the continent within the shortest possible time. They can change the economy, the lifestyle and standard of living of people. Like I said earlier, with almost 80 million people actively going to church in Nigeria, there is no excuse in the world why the country should be near comatose. When we have even if it is 20 million people actively converting and living in an engaging manner for a year, Nigeria will begin to pride herself in the community of developed nations.

That is the kind of spirituality that I understand. God made his own spirituality visible. God made all the things we see, he made them tangible and they came out of his spirituality. The heavens declare his glory, the stars all came out of the spirituality of God. The air, the oxygen and all that we enjoy came out of his spirituality and he made them all visible.

How is your spirituality being made visible and being demonstrated?

The Bible says that how God anointed Jesus Christ of Nazareth with the Holy Ghost and with power that he went about doing good. No one wants to go about doing good today, people want to stay in church and live there. Everyone wants to build a church and receive offerings.

The proof of the anointing of Jesus was that he was going about making his anointing visible by doing good. He was converting the anointing to visible actions, attributes, functions, events and manifestations. He was converting all the anointing, making it visible and going about looking for how much good he could still do. He was converting the anointing into physical good, into health, into salvation, into strength, into hope, into life, he was converting it into food and going about doing good. We have to see the result of your anointing and it must not just be on the pulpit. He touched people, he did physical things, he paid his taxes.

Hebrews 11:3 says through faith we understand...Faith when converted is converted into understanding. This understanding is what all men will come into.

So the things that are not seen must be made into something seen.

ALL THINGS MUST BE CONVERTED BEFORE THEY BENEFIT THE EARTH

The faith you have must create something seen. Love is not seen but it must make something tangible and be seen, it must be converted into good works like Mother Theresa. She had love but it meant nothing until it was converted.

Faith, hope must all be converted. I want to see the result of your invisible faith.

Everything we see right now came from invisible things. Power and prophecy must be brought to visibility for it to be relevant on the earth. It must become tangible. Faith without works is dead. Your faith must be worked out into some visible manifestations. Your experiences and also your religiosity. Jesus was anointed and converted that into going about, and doing good. He converted it into healing and deliverance and was busy using invisible power and anointing to cause physical benefits for all humanity to enjoy.

That is what Bill gates and Steve Jobs have done and all the people we ridicule as unbelievers. Satan does not create iPads and computers. They have been able to bring the benefits of the spiritual realm into tangible products.

Even though these are all spiritual blessings, Christians are not catching them. For you to catch a thing from the spirit, you must have a developed mind. Even though you have goose bumps, it won't be converted until you have understanding, intellect and insight. This is why the Bill Gates, Steve Jobs and Mark Zukerberg are the ones converting.

They get ideas and they convert them into products we all benefit from today.

John 1:1 states *'In the beginning was the word and the word was with God'...*

Even though the word was there in the beginning and he was God, it didn't benefit anyone on the earth. Anything that is not physically manifested and tangibly manifested is not of benefit to anyone on the earth.

The word that was there from the beginning as powerful as it was could not benefit anyone until it became flesh. It could benefit no one until it dwelt among us and we beheld his glory. It benefited us when we could behold him. We could experience eternal life and salvation because he became manifested.

This wouldn't have happened if he wasn't manifested. Only manifested things have benefit on the earth. Even though God wanted to save the earth, the only way even God could help us is to become converted by making his word become flesh. God had to convert from spirit to flesh and into this physical and material realm for him to save us. His love had to become converted into something tangible. Your own relationship with God has to become converted into something tangible. Your spirituality must be converted into something physical for it to become beneficial.

Only when God himself subjected himself to this principle did he benefit the world. He made this order and principle and he will not violate this order and principle.

THERE IS NEED TO TAKE RESPONSIBILITY

In Nigeria for example, we perhaps have more Churches per square meter than any other country in the world, it will not benefit anyone anything until we learn conversion. We will keep getting more impoverished the more spiritual we become. Our politicians will become the worst in the world, our doctors a mess, our engineers dummies simply because we are not converting into tangible physical manifestation.

We are not producing goods and services, we are not releasing people to go explore the world of science. We have become like the Dark Age churches just talking irrelevant spirituality. The world no longer becomes like the kingdom of heaven but like hell because we refuse to become the kingdom of heaven but hell. Jesus' prayer was thy kingdom come. It is our responsibility to make sure his kingdom comes into our families, our homes, our streets, our markets, our world. If we are not doing that we are bringing hell. We are responsible, we are the ones to blame for the way our country has become. We are not taking responsibility for the militants, the kidnappers, the prostitutes through our so called anointing.

We are not converting the earth into heaven and as long as we are running away from the earth, hell will continue to invade the earth and heaven will continue to be far from the earth. Yes, and we will only taste heaven when we die. God wants us to taste heaven on earth and that is what we are supposed to be busy about. We should show all men what is obtainable in heaven and show everyone on the earth.

GOLDEN NUGGETS
FROM CHAPTER 5

- Christians need to be taught all over again how to live on earth.

- Anytime an authority, for example religious authority tries to silence the people, it always leads to backwardness and dark ages.

- If you are not converting all of your spirituality into material benefits, it is a waste of time.

- The things in heaven that we try to escape into must be transferred to this earth.

- Only tangible things benefit people on earth. The earth is meant for only physical tangible things.

- Our calling is supposed to be in the world with real tangible results.

- Without fruit, church going becomes a waste of time. We want to see the result of what you have done or achieved.

CHAPTER 6

HOW TO LIVE THE BEST LIFE, THE SUPERIMPOSING LIFESTYLE

If you want to lead an extraordinary life,
find out what the ordinary do–and don't
do it.

TOMMY NEWBERRY

This topic is very intriguing. This chapter also is very critical to your existence on earth. In this chapter we will be discussing how to live the best life in this world, the super imposing lifestyle. The best life for me is when you are able to live the superimposing lifestyle.

When you are able to live a lifestyle of superimposition, then you are living the best life. I'm hoping that after this chapter, your eyes will be opened for you to know that you can live the supernatural life, but also a superimposing life. Your life can be unique, your life can be out of the ordinary. A life that you can be proud of. A life like Jesus. This is what I'm going to show you. A super human life is possible on the basis of the lifestyle of Jesus. How did Jesus live that life and how can we live such a life too?

LIVING THE SUPERIMPOSING LIFESTYLE

Now, the Bible says about Jesus that He was the first born of the brethren. He was not just a God in the flesh. While he was on earth, he was 100% human. Why God allowed him to be 100% human was to be human like us, to be as close to us as possible. God allowed him to go through all that we go through and to experience all that we experience and live the super imposing life as an example for us.

Another reason why he was 100% human is because God also wanted to put us on equal footing. That means Jesus would be like us. It also meant we will know that which made him supernatural. What made Jesus supernatural was not that he was the son of God or the second in the trinity. It was because he was human with the spirit of God in him. We too are human but with the spirit of God in us. That makes us to be on equal footing and hence we can desire to live as he lived.

We have the 100% flesh like Jesus and the spirit of God which is 100% God. That actually made Jesus the first born of the brethren. All of us that were born after him are also children of God and were born as junior brothers and sisters to Jesus. He was the first born and we are his brothers and sisters. If he, as the senior brother was able to live the superimposing life, we too as God's children can live as he lived.

HOW TO LIVE THE SUPERIMPOSING LIFE

How does this work? It is in knowing why Jesus came. Jesus came to give us a model and a prototype of how the best life could be lived. His life was a demonstration of that life being possible. He came to show us that it is possible to live our lives pleasing the lord completely in every way. A life that is so close to Jesus and is comparable to the way Jesus lived.

Jesus was our model of the super imposing life and he came to show us how to live the best of life. What is that best life and how did he show us how to live such a life?

John 5:19-20 explains to us

"Most assuredly, I say to you, the Son can do nothing of Himself, but what He sees the Father do; for whatever He does, the Son also does in like manner. For the Father loves the Son, and shows Him all things that He Himself does; and He will show Him greater works than these, that you may marvel."

Also John 6:38 states "For I have come down from heaven, not to do my own will, but the will of Him who sent me."

The best life to live on earth by any human being is the ability to find out what the father is thinking. The best life is to be obsessed with what ideas are in the mind of the father. The super-imposing life is to be possessed by God's thoughts and what impressions are on his mind.

God is our ultimate example and model, we came from him and are created in his image and likeness. Our life is a reflection and replica of his life. The ultimate duplication and copy and imitation that we should have is the imitation of God. We will live the best life if we can live our life imitating his ultimate life and model and prototype. Our ultimate example model and original is God.

It has been told us that he made us to be his copy and likeness and image. That is quite clear. For us to be able to imitate him better, Jesus came to live in same circumstances on earth. He came to demonstrate to us that such a life is possible. He reflected and modeled out for us how one can live in the flesh and still live the life of the original, the creator's standard and the ultimate ideal life. The ideal life is God's life and such a life could be imitated and lived on the earth.

Jesus came and showed us how to go about such a life. He did it and it worked out for him so that we will not doubt anymore. He lived an exemplary life so that we can live the life of God on earth in the midst of Satan and sin, death and destruction. Our lives can still reflect God's life on earth.

WHAT PROCESS CAN WE FOLLOW TO GET TO THE BEST LIFE?

Again the best life is to be able to live in accordance to the original. Anything you see today, iPad and phones, gadgets and products are copies of the original and each of them is an original. An original copy can only be at best a copy of the real original. what do I mean? What I am trying to say is that you cannot have the best copy of another copy. The best copy an object can be is of the original.

We are humans and are copies of God. We are replicas of God and the best thing we could do and the best life we can be is the life that is closest to the original. A life that is closest to the example. A life that is closest to the prototype. The prototype is God. He had the best life, the ultimate life in Himself. The best life to live therefore is that life that reflects the closest reflection of God. A life that duplicates the best. The better you duplicate God, the better your life on earth. The best life on earth is the life that most effectively duplicates, reflects, and replicates the original life.

On a daily basis, to live the best life means to find out what are the things in the mind of the master. In technology, what are the things on his mind? In telecommunications, in the area of industry, and developments of the world, in medicine, in economy, what are the next inventions on God's mind in the movie, in entertainments, in the fashion world? What is God trying to bring about in your nation and government, what ideas will God birth to solve war, hunger and poverty in the world.

The closer I am in discovering those things, the better I am. The closer I am to God to decipher what thoughts are going on in God's mind in those areas, the better I am able to reach and stretch into his mind and bring out those things down into the earth. That is the best life. That is the best form of life anyone can possibly live on the earth. It is this form of life that gives meaning to your existence on this planet.

You can live the best life as regards what God wants to do in church life, but you may not be living the best life in the world of your calling. You must know how God wants you to live in the area of your calling. God is infinite, he is omnipotent, all powerful. It is impossible to exhaust God. You can only decipher to a large extent in the area of your calling and in a certain sphere of life. Even when you have exhausted all that there is to exhaust in the world of your calling, you would only have touched a bit of God. It is in that area of your calling where you are able to reflect God and that you are able to decipher what he wants to do, his intentions, his purpose, his ideas and the plans of what he wants to do in your world and concerning your nation. You will be able to see what he wants and you can bring that to the earth and implement it on the earth. When you live like that, you are living the best of life.

LIVING OUT THE BEST FORM OF LIFE

The best life is the ability to see the original life, the prototype life and the model life. The best life is seeing into your area of strength, gifting and calling and seeing what God is communicating. The best life begins when you live out the instructions of God. You must transfix and see into the spirit realm, labor mentally and project that which you see. You must then communicate what you see into the real world and bring it into the physical tangible products that everyone can understand.

Only then is your light shining and everyone will be able to see and the people of the world can testify to seeing your light. You have made your ideas and energy palpable, palatable and comprehensible to people. You have seen what God is doing and what actions he is taking and you have brought this down for everyone to benefit and enjoy.

This is establishing the kingdom reality on earth. That is the interpretation of thy kingdom come, thy will be done on earth. The whole essence of that request and desire is to bring the kingdom to earth and to establish the kingdom here. This is the best way to live life and that is the superimposing life.

THE BEST LIFE REFLECTS HEAVEN'S REALITY ON EARTH

The superimposing life is the life that is over and above the earth, the life that goes through the spirit realm. You go into heaven to bring understanding and insight and ideas from there, then you are using those ideas and concepts to superimpose the earth. Those ideas are used as a blanket for everyone, they have no choice but to obey the will of heaven. That is a life that is superior to the life on the earth. That is a life that is coming from above.

That life is used to control the earth, imposing the God life and kingdom life from above and over the realities of the earth. You are no longer coming under the control of those things that should come under you. You are not under the control of elements and situations and circumstances on the earth. Rather, you are living your life in accordance with the agenda of heaven. You are directly imposing God's and heaven's will and vision upon your world. The world is not putting you under, controlling and captivating you and making you live the way it wants. The best life is to be able to reach into the spirit, connect with God and get the picture of what God wants. The best life is to understand his thinking and thought, connect with that will and bring that will into colorful and wonderful realities on earth. The best life is to bring into everyone's experience heaven's realities, imposing those realities into everyone's realities upon the earth. It is the best form of life that is possible. This is why we need Christianity.

THE PURPOSE OF CHRISTIANITY

The purpose of Christianity is to be able to live the super imposing lifestyle. To be able to gain access into heaven's realm. And to be able to bring God's thoughts to the earth.

We must be able to duplicate and replicate the ultimate example and the experience and atmosphere of heaven on the earth. We must bring it all to the earth and be able to see the reality of the original. We must be able to connect to heaven. We must see on regular basis and have the capacity to transfer the reality of what obtains over there. We must develop what we see through understanding and by wisdom implement them into real life experiences on earth.

That way the calamities of the world will not be ruling over us. The tragedies and the problems on earth will be beyond our reach. You will be standing over and above the earth and all its circumstances. You will be establishing upon the earth something that is coming from above. This must be the teaching in every church. Every church should help you in strengthening your relationship with God. They must help you access the resources of the spirit realm. You must be able to hear, see and understand and also be able to bring heaven to the earth. Jesus said we must pray to be that instrument that God's Kingdom come, and that his will be done on earth as it is in heaven.

You must be able to have intimacy with God in order to do this. You must be able to walk one on one with God. You must be able to see and to understand what God wants. You cannot go to a church where you are not being taught how to walk and have a personal relationship with God. The problem begins when the church is religious and when the church no longer teaches how to have a personal walk with God. When we lack how to walk with God individually and on a personal basis, egocentrism is born.

When you are not taught how to be close with God, you are living a religious, empty life. Such life is irrelevant on earth. Some are basically living just to go to heaven when rather heaven wants to invade the earth through you. The major message on our pulpits are merely religious.

Signs and wonders, miracles and prosperity, healing and breakthroughs will produce nothing in people than emptiness. You are not taught how to be a friend of God, how to access God's mind and how to transfer and superimpose his will on the earth. You are hardly taught how to make his kingdom come to earth.

It is easier for people who know God to be able to make their environment look like heaven. The countries we live in should reflect heaven. Only by seeing heaven and downloading heaven's experiences by wisdom unto the earth can this happen. We must be able to bring heaven to the earth and implement heaven on earth. Until this world becomes the kingdom of our God and of his son Christ.

This is why John 3:31 states *"The one who comes from above is above all; the one who is from the earth belongs to the earth, and speaks as one from the earth. The one who comes from heaven is above all."*

You understand that now. Even though we are still here on earth, the real way we are to live on earth is the way of the super imposing lifestyle. The super imposing lifestyle is in that scripture.

When you come from above, you are above all circumstances, all situations, conditions, state of affairs, all things. When you come from above, you are above all positions; all events and turns of events. Incidents, occurrences and happenings have no power over you.

When you are a friend of God, you have intimacy with God, you have access into heaven. When you can seek the father, you can love the father. You have intimacy with the father, you love the father and understand the father's heart.

You will know his will in every aspect of life, agriculture, media, road, infrastructure, sports, entertainment, communication, construction etc because these are all aspects of God. He is all encompassing.

Only with a personal walk with God can you live super imposingly.

It is only those who though their body are here but have a personal walk with God that can live the super imposing lifestyle. Only those who are in friendship and intimacy with God. Only people who are close to God are able to live the super imposing lifestyle because they are coming from over and above.

Such people are in the spirit and have spiritual understanding. They know the experiences God wants for the earth. They are eager to come to the earth to subdue it and to superimpose that will of God and that desire of God in his heart. They have the perfect aspirations in the heart of God. They know his yearnings, they are busy converting what they saw in the spirit, building and constructing their vision of God and of heaven on earth.

They want to change the reality on earth to reflect the reality of heaven. They are busy with God to find out his will and what he wants to do on earth. They are working with God to interpret his mind into the language of men so that everyone can understand it and bring glory to their father in heaven. This is why Christianity was founded. It was to bring you intimacy and personal relationship with God for everyone to have that personal walk and relationship with

God too. To download God's intention into every sphere of life.

This is the brand of Christianity to engage in. The emphasis is not on signs, miracles, heaven etc. It should be intimacy with God, a personal walk with God, friendship with God etc. You are so intimate with God you can see him and with a developed mind and can understand what God wants to do on the earth.

When you live like that you qualify for the experience described in John 3:31.

HOW TO LIVE FROM GOD'S PERSPECTIVE

When you live from God's perspective, you live the superimposing lifestyle.

You come from above when your perspectives are different. Your world view and your paradigms reflect more of heaven and kingdom and what is obtainable in heaven than what is available on the earth. When your actions on earth are being dictated by heaven as against the things that are on the earth, then you are living a superimposing lifestyle on the earth. You are bringing the will of God to pass on the earth. That is the best life and it means to come from above.

It doesn't mean you are above in the flesh. No, it only means your paradigm, world view, motivation, inspiration, actions, your ideas, your values are based on what you have seen. Your preoccupation is to bring to pass what you have seen and observed. When you live like that, it means you have come from above. When you live like that, it means you are coming from above.

The Bible says those that are of the earth are earthly. Their motivation and preoccupation and day to day routine is what obtains on the earth and what is of the earth. The circumstances of the earth influences them. They are earthly, their motivation and their pursuit is earthly. They speak like the people on the earth, their inspirations are the inspirations of others.

This is why many preachers speak the same things, many are absent from the fathers heart to know what God is saying or to get fresh bread. Many preachers just spice other preachers' sermons and revelations of others with a tint of their own charisma. They lack revelation and make God look like he is dead and has nothing new for his people. Many churches hire ideas from the world to make their churches more interesting than others. The reason is because they lack revelation of heaven. The earth is influencing many lives and churches than they are being influenced by heaven. They lack anything new from God. The core of most churches is same. Their motivation is earth. People are not connected to heaven to receive fresh bread.

God is always trying to pass across something new, God is always working and if you will constantly download from God's heart you must be intimate with God. This is why we must all return to the message of intimacy with God and personal relationship with heaven so that everyone will be able to superimpose on the earth their revelations of heaven.

He that comes from heaven always wins, he will always win. When your thoughts and ideas are from heaven, there is no way you will not be the best, the head, the first. You cannot be the tail or the last. When your strategy is divine, you cannot fail because you are living the superimposing lifestyle.

We are not the best in technology, medicine, music, comedy, entertainment for lack of the superimposing life-style. We are just living like mere men, like ordinarily men when God says we are gods.

We must superimpose on medicine, on politics, on technology. His mind, his thoughts, his pictures, his image and ideas must be made to reflect in literature, in governance, in our educational systems etc

Even if we are close enough, we need a developed mind to understand the scenes and pictures we get from God. With a developed mind we interpret what we see in the spirit. When the mind is not developed, we cannot properly understand and communicate these ideas and make it applicable on the earth. Only things that are understood are applicable and can be converted.

THE CHURCH MUST SHIFT

The church must not remain beggarly, religious, bent as if we don't have access to God. We cannot just exist as every other religious group or institution on earth. He that is earthly speaks like the earth but he that is from heaven speaks heavenly and reveals heaven to earth. The ideas and thoughts are from the heart of the father, they are fresh and will super impose the earth.

Remember, I said Jesus showed us how to live this kind of life and that was why he came. The church must follow this example, we must be like Jesus. Let us look at an example of how he did it.

In John 6: 38, when he said he came from heaven it is not just physically. When he said that he meant his source, his origin, his motivation, his paradigm, the origin of his actions and mentality, his source of power and why he thinks and behaves differently are from heaven. He said he did not come to do his own will on the earth. If that is true of Jesus, same is true of us, His church.

All his projects, miracles etc are not coming from the earth. He is not living from the earth on the earth. He is living from heaven on the earth. His thoughts, projects and ideas are coming from above. He's always connected and hooked up to the father. He's always going away to separate himself and to build intimacy with God and to see what God is seeing.

The purpose of prayer and walk with God is to be able to see what the father is seeing and willing to do on the earth. The purpose of our lives is to live out that which is pressing on the father's heart and that which he is willing to bring about. What the father is willing to do on the earth comes from such alone moments to implement what he is seeing, He is now living from the above down on the earth. He is coming from above into situations and circumstances, hence he sees differently and speaks differently.

The lifestyle we are supposed to be living is the lifestyle that makes us see into the mind of God all the time and to convert what we see in the situations and circumstances happening on the earth. When in heaven we do not see lack, we must implement same on the earth.

Jesus said he is not doing his own will and he is not just doing what he wants to do. He said he has come to do the will of He who sent him. Jesus is showing us the secret. If we are to live the best life, we must live the will of the father. We must constantly be connected to the father and his will and be dedicated to bring down the will through conversion, understanding and bringing down the tangible reality on earth. The will of the father is the invisible part. It is the invisible part, but we know his will by what Jesus did because he converted the intangible will of God into tangible reality upon the earth. He converted it into lifestyles and miraculous events. He imposed what he saw into earth's circumstances.

When Lazarus was sick, he already saw that the sickness was not unto death. So when Lazarus was dead, he could say let's go wake him.

As scientists, inventors, preachers, writers, artisans, business leaders etc, we are supposed to be connected to the invisible ideas, knowledge, start-ups, know how, strategies. We must be connected to all that is in God and must be connected in the spirit. Through our mind, we convert those things into visible tangible products on the earth. That's the super imposing lifestyle which is the best life on earth.

AS I SEE I DO

Jesus said again that he cannot do anything except the things he sees the father doing.

He has to see some things first, he has to gain some revelation first. Jesus refused to be motivated by the earth, he refused to be instigated by the earth, he refused to do what everyone does. He even refused to marry because his motivation for such was different. People were doing all they wished, but he was doing differently because his perspective and source was different. Once he sees what the father is doing, that becomes his obsession and he begins to build it into tangible things that will make all men glorify God.

That was how Jesus' life became superlative and superimposing.

Jesus also said in John 5: 30, *"I can of mine own self do nothing: as I hear, I judge: and my judgment is just; because I seek not mine own will, but the will of the Father which hath sent me."*

Again, what he hears from heaven is not from the earth. He hears from heaven and lets it connect to his mind. He then converts by wisdom what he has heard into products and hard work. He went about doing good, making it into the reality of men's experiences. We must understand this formula and use this same formula. We must download always and convert what we hear into tangible products and reality on the earth.

As I hear, I judge and my judgment is just. He said he seeks not his own will. He was always seeking to deny himself and was always connected to download. He was always making sure he was busy all the time. All the things he spoke were those things he had sought and found in the fathers will.

You have to seek it, that's why you need personal time with God. This does not translate to going to church. Going to Church can be a distraction to your personal walk with God. Though going to church may also enhance your personal relationship, many have not found it beneficial to their close walk with God.

Your ultimate goal should be to develop your walk with God. To see what God sees and to dedicate your life, time and energy to bring about all that God is showing to you. This is the superimposing lifestyle. Using the reality of heaven to blanket the earth and change realities on the earth. That is why everything on the earth has a tone in heaven. You must seek to understand what is happening in the spirit now and be able to bring that into physical tangible manifestations.

We have this opportunity. In Ephesians 2:6, we understood that God (He) has raised us from the dead along with Christ and seated us with him in the heavenly realms because we are united with Christ Jesus.

In the spirit realm, we are already sitting in the right hand of the Father in the heavenly places. From there we can superimpose the realities of God upon the earth.

In the spirit, we are to see ourselves sitting at the right hand of the father, walking and seeing what he sees and seeking to do that which we are seeing into what everyone else can see.

When we convert and everyone sees this, they will glorify our father who is in heaven.

Jesus was so strong and emphatic about this that he said, if I do not do this, if you find a fraction of the earth in me, you don't have to believe.

Jesus was a workaholic, very busy to convert all that he saw into physical and tangible things because only physical tangible things can be relevant upon the earth. Somebody had to convert God's idea on the earth and that was what Jesus did through work.

He said his work was to do the will of God. He had to convert the invisible will into physical tangible results through hard work. He had to convert from the spirit into physical manifestations. He taught us to do same and to pray 'thy will be done on earth'. We can do this when we devote to a thorough life of hard work.

My dear friend, it is my earnest desire to see you live the best life, the super-imposing life. It is God's desire for you to live the supernatural life on the earth. I implore you to refuse to be normal, ordinary and of no consequence. You must desire to see what the father sees and work to bring it into physical realities on the earth.

GOLDEN NUGGETS
FROM CHAPTER 6

- The best life on earth is when you are able to live the superimposing lifestyle.

- What made Jesus supernatural was not that he was the son of God or the second in the trinity. It was because he was human with the spirit of God in him.

- The super-imposing life is to be possessed by God's thoughts and what impressions are on his mind.

- It is tragic to live the best life as regards what God wants to do in church life, but not to live the best life in the world of your calling.

- The best life is seeing into your area of strength, gifting and calling and seeing what God is communicating.

- When we lack how to walk with God individually and on a personal basis, egocentrism is born.

- The purpose of prayer and walk with God is to be able to see what the father is seeing and willing to do on the earth.

CHAPTER 7

THE BIRTH OF RELIGION

If Jesus came back and saw what was being done in his name, he'd never stop throwing up.
WOODY ALLEN

Throughout this book, we have consistently seen that the bane of conversion is religion. What is religion and where did it come from? Religion comes from people who are so focused on getting things done for themselves. It comes from people who are so focused on their needs, they go to God with the intention of using him to meet their own needs. Once they get their way, they stay in that building using God just for their needs.

Put more accurately, religion is Christianity when it stops converting. When you go to 'church', pray but lack a relationship with God, you are merely practicing religion. Religion is tradition and culture rather than relationship. When you go to church every Sunday and also during the week just to show up as a routine, that's religion. Are you scared of your Church leaders or live in fear of what people will say if you do other than their expectations, then it means you are caught up in tradition and empty religion.

If you go to church just because you have some problems and you need God to solve them, that is religion.

If you go to church for any reason other than to be able to convert the knowledge of God into something practical to benefit others and your environment , then that is pure religion.

RELIGION STARTS WHERE CONVERSION STOPS

The start of mere religion is putting a stop to conversion. In other words, religion starts where conversion stops. That is a good statement right there.

If your religious experience remains only an experience and that experience is not converted, then you are now in religion and not in a relationship. It means your faith is now dead because faith without works is dead.

Faith without works is religion. When faith is no more working and being actively converted, it becomes dead. It means you are no more actively converting what you know about God. You must work to convert what you know about God and it is through works that your faith can be converted. The reason why our faith must be worked out is for it to be converted.

Every time you claim to be a Christian and believer, it means you are converting your faith into substance. If that is not happening, you really do not have faith, what you have is dead religion.

So my question to you today is 'how intense is the process of conversion going with your faith? Are you constantly in the process of conversion? That is, are you converting whatever you discover about God? Is your faith mingled with works? If you are not coming out with products from your faith, then you are not converting it. Without conversion, you are stuck with religion.

So you need to question yourself if what you have is engaging conversion. Whenever our walk with God and our knowledge of him is not being converted into real valuable substance for people, countries and the kingdom of God, we are only practicing religion. That means our faith is without work.

FAITH WITHOUT WORKS IS RELIGION

Your faith must be worked out, you must always work on your faith. You must always do something to work out what you have discovered about God. You must always find ways to convert your faith into something tangible. You must always convert your faith.

Let me show you how I got to know about this;

When your faith stops giving forth results, in the sense that you are not working it out, then it means that you are now a religious person not a believer. Jesus always confronted this when he was on earth, especially with his disciples.

Man would rather be religious than be productive. Most Christians would rather be religious than be believers.

We don't want to constantly work on our faith. Our lazy nature seems to always take over and take the better side of us, no matter how actively we began.

The disciples struggled so much with this when Christ was with them. Christ always fought it with them because he did not want them to become religious. He rebuked them when they failed to convert what they learnt from him because he knew they would become religious on those things. Thus he kept on rebuking these disciples.

Let us look at this instance when they were not ready to convert and would rather go religious.

In John 14: 8-11, Phillip said to Jesus, *"Lord, show us the Father, and it is sufficient for us."*

Jesus said to him, *"Have I been with you so long, and yet you have not known Me, Philip?"*

He who has seen me has seen the Father; so how can you say, 'Show us the Father'? Do you not believe that I am in the Father, and the Father in Me? The words that I speak to you I do not speak on my own authority; but the Father who dwells in me does the works. Believe me that I am in the Father and the Father in Me, or else believe me for the sake of the works themselves.

Though Phillip had been around Jesus, yet he had not known him. We can say he had been in church but he had not discovered God. It is possible to attend Church several times a week but not know or discover God. How many people in churches today can you say have discovered God for themselves? Many go to Churches without discovering God for themselves. The visits many pay to church weekly have not been converted into a personal relationship with God.

THERE IS NEED FOR SELF-ASSESSMENT

Has your own going to Church been converted into a personal relationship with God? Your church going and weekly attendance in Church meetings must be converted. You must ask yourself, is this church going helping me to convert? What has my church attendance helped me to produce yet? Who has my religiosity, my bible reading and praying been of benefit to? Have all these activities been converted into the knowledge of God? If the answer is no, then you know you are in trouble.

Now is the time to stop and ask yourself, 'what are those religious activities that I have been engaged in that are not converting into a genuine relationship with God and into discovering God. Make a list so you can know those things that did not make you discover, know and walk personally and intimately with God. You have to now say to yourself that they are not helping your walk with God, they are only birthing religion in my psyche. I don't need to engage in them anymore.

Judge your visits to mountains and attendance at several prayer meetings by how much intimacy it has brought into your personal walk with God. How much intimacy have those activities brought to your personal walk with God?

How much knowledge and personal experience has it brought to you. Have those experiences brought you to a place where you can say that you know God better and you know how to please him?

Many people write to me explaining that two months of listening to my messages has made them know more of themselves and of God. To such people, more of God has been revealed to them within a very short time than in the years they have spent in Church engaging in fruitless religious activities.

Can you believe that?

Critically analyze your life because if your Christianity and church going is not bringing about conversion. If you are not converting your religiosity into personal relationship with God, then you are just wasting your life. If you are not converting your religiosity into knowledge of God and intimacy with God, you are wasting your life.

THE MONSTER CALLED RELIGION

Religion kills because it has no life in it. That is the birth of religion! Whenever you stop converting your religious experiences, you give birth to a monster. Religion has pushed many people into busying themselves with what other people are wearing, what others are eating basically busying themselves with other people's affairs.

Religion gives birth to monsters called gossip, control, comparison, jealousy and so on. Religion makes some people think others are better than them or that they are better than others. Those are monsters that religion gives birth to as a result of lack of conversion.

Any time conversion ends, religion begins. Religious activities give you pregnancy even if you don't want one.

Whenever you refuse to practice all that you have been taught, you end up with religion.

People can come to church and still be religious because it is a personal decision to convert. Others in a congregation may cause you to be religious when you are being pushed and pressured to do things. Religion makes you engage in activities because of other people. When you stop going to church because of others, that is also religion, it is also akin to religion.

THE PURPOSE OF RELIGIOUS ACTIVITIES

Religious activities should be targeted at getting to know more of God.

Whenever you undertake any religious program, it should be because you want to discover more of God, you want to discover more about him every day.

In the scripture we considered earlier, Philip was getting religious even under Jesus, he was getting pregnant with the evil monster of Religion. Jesus was amazed that Philip had not even known him.

The most important essence of anything we do as believers should be to know God. That is why Apostle Paul cried out 'That I may know him...

That should also be your desire. Not that you may get your breakthrough or just that you may get your needs met, but that you may know him.

The desire to know him must be paramount and must be the number one thing. If your church going is not helping you with that, then you should advise yourself. Jesus said where two or three are gathered in his name...that means it is sometimes better to just be with your own family and get to discover GOD or with just a few friends who can help you to discover God and become like God.

THE BUILDING IS NOT CHURCH.

Church is where you are brought closer to personal discovery and you strengthen your personal walk with God.

Church is where your knowledge of God is enhanced and your relationship with God is strengthened.

In fact fellowshipping with God with a book in the hand might be a better form of worship than what some people have in church buildings.

Anything that brings you to a personal relationship with God that is Church. And if you are going to a building that is not bringing you newness and helping you build a firm relationship, it is not church.

Church must bring you a personal relationship greater than just religious activities do. You are supposed to eliminate all the activities you are involved in today that is not bringing you closer to God. Eliminate all that is not helping you walk with God. That was what Jesus was telling his disciples. He was rebuking him. He was confronting Philip's comfort. Phillip was getting comfortable and Jesus rebuked that.

That is what many of us do today, we only go to church to warm up and enjoy ourselves, we attend services to feel good and get comfortable. We attend services to enjoy the time and enjoy good music. If you attend Church just for some good music, you are already impregnated with an unwanted pregnancy called religion. You are already birthing religion if your motive of going to church is just for the atmosphere or because your language is being spoken there and majority of the people are from your nationality.

If you go to Church for culture sake, you have birthed the monster called religion. That was what Jesus fought in that passage that we read.

He said Philip was around him probably because he got food, or because he felt good or maybe because of miracles. His presence around Jesus could have been just for the companionship and friendship. Jesus said he would rather leave or convert.

What conversion was Jesus talking about here? He was telling him to convert his Presence and closeness and proximity into real knowledge of God. Religious activities must bring us into real knowledge of God. He had been with Jesus but he had not seen God. We can be in church and not see God, we can be within the church building and not know God. We may engage in activities and not see God, we can even preach about God, yet not know him.

RELIGION IS NOT THE SAME AS KNOWLEDGE OF GOD

There are so many preachers with no idea of who God is. You can be a preacher and have no sense of God. The church may make you a Pastor, but it cannot force you to know God.

Being in church does not make you a believer, going for Sunday programs does not make you a believer, even preaching does not make you know God.

What do you think happened to Philip? He was in the presence of God for years yet could not identify who God was. He was in the presence of Jesus and was still asking the way to God. What level of ignorance! He lacked the idea of who Jesus was. This is how religion could blind you, it could blind your eyes and deafen your ears. Religion is a deafener. Religion could make you blind because here we see an example of it where Philip was totally blind to the realities of God. God was there in front of him, yet he could not see. Religion was a fog covering his eyes not to see Christ.

Your religious activities can be mere activities, you can do things daily and it will amount to nothing. When you do not act and you fail to convert, that is mere head knowledge. You lack faith and the presence of God. You must learn to convert your proximity with God and activities into personal knowledge of God and closeness with God.

Jesus said *'I have been so long here...'*

You could sleep in church or live in the Pastor's house, you could even be the wife of the Pastor and still not know God.

Jesus was surprised and replied 'You have not known Me Philip...

The goal of our activities is to see God. The goal of our religious activities is to see him and to know him. I have books, audio/video messages on my blog (Sundayadela-jablog.com) and YouTube channel (Sunday Adelaja Official) on prayers and you will do well to thoroughly go through them.

They will teach you how to discover yourself and how to convert prayers into seeing God and hearing God. It is possible to pray and not see God and one of the purposes of our prayers is to see God.

The purpose of our activities is to be able to see the father. That is the problem that Philip had. He was seeing Jesus as human, as ordinary, he could not see in the spirit. He was not connecting in the spirit and using his spiritual eyes. He was not seeing beyond the body and the physical things he was experiencing.

Many of us are just like Phillip, he was just after what he could get. Our intention should not be about what we would get, our passion should be to know God and to discover God for ourselves. Our priority should not be what to eat, what to wear and where to live because when these are your priorities, you get blinded.

Our personal relationship must not be built on needs being met but on the desire to know him, to discover him, to fellowship with him and have a personal relationship with him. Philip's focus was not on intimacy and he missed it.

THE WAYS OF GOD VERSUS THE WORKS OF GOD

Miracles could be a distraction and because you are so taken away by it that you never discover the miracle worker. The children of Israel saw the miracles but they never saw the miracle worker. That is still what is happening today.

Moses knew the way of God, he saw God and he was more particular about knowing God, knowing his principles. That makes the difference between men whom God used and the rest of the people. While real men seek God, the crowd are following for his acts, for bread.

It is futile to go to churches where every emphasis is laid on miracles rather than on principles. Miracles may fill you for a period of time but not forever. The men who ate the bread Jesus multiplied got hungry again and started looking for him. That is what many people do with all their time and the whole of their life.

I get sad when I see people drawn not by the ways of God but the works of God, It is embarrassing and it's a disgrace. Most people flock into churches in Africa because of miracles and it becomes a criteria why many choose what church to go to.

Just recently, in 2016 specifically, a man named Penuel Mnguni, an acclaimed 24 year old controversial South African Prophet who made his followers eat snakes in his church saying that he had turned them into a chocolate just like Jesus did with water and wine in the bible died after being bitten by a cobra he was using for another round of miracles in his Ministry.

The South African prophet rose to international fame in just weeks after he rode his congregants like donkeys, made them strip naked in church, eat their own hair braids or that of others. He also made his congregants eat materials like paper, rocks, and dirt. He shocked the entire world when he brought live snakes to his services, and declared that those who believed in the power of Jesus and had faith could eat the venomous snakes and God would turn them to chocolate.

Congregants who munched on the animals claimed that the snakes indeed tasted like chocolate to them. The prophet quickly became known as the 'Snake Pastor' in South Africa, where gained attention and popularity.

My heart bleeds when I come in contact with stories like this. Why? This is the level of abasement and degradation that the human mind can become subjected to in the name of seeking miracles. How else will you describe the behavior of eating grass, drinking ridiculous substances, buying anointing clothing and materials, sowing your salary as seeds which they make you believe is your 'first fruit', 'prophet's seed', 'break through seed', 'seed of escape', and

RAISING THE NEXT GENERATION OF STEVE JOBS AND BILL GATES

other very ridiculous practices? How do you convince me such behavior is not animalistic? Which other word do you use for the people involved if not gullible? All of such acts are paganist and anti-God. You perish when you spend your life chasing miracles, chasing shadows. Even Lazarus that was raised by Jesus himself from the dead still died eventually and nobody raised him p again. Miracles must not be the hall mark of your life, principles and responsibility must be the hall mark of your life.

There was once an event which shook the media rooms of the world in 1981. In the small town of Medjugorje in what is now Bosnia-Herzegovina, six children reported seeing appearances of the Virgin Mary. For years they claimed to receive daily messages and so far have allegedly received thousands of prophecies from Virgin Mary.

You know what was surprising to me and to some people in the world? The site immediately began attracting millions of people from around the world who saw the place as some holy place and began to go on pilgrimage there to offer prayers for miracles.

The gullibility of the human mind appalls me and scares me. Before you blame all the people who immediately began going to these sites, ask yourself what you would do if such a thing suddenly appears in your city tomorrow. What would you do when a man, a miracle merchant suddenly appears who claims to have all the power for miracles and blessings? Oh, perhaps right now you are even a candi-

THE BIRTH OF RELIGION

date of such places? Unfortunately, that is what majority of churches in Africa have become.

We do not only destroy ourselves when we engage in gullible acts like these and miracle adventures, we in essence destroy humanity and destroy the world.

Principles and the truth of God's word must be your priority. People who are interested in miracles perish in the wilderness of life because they failed to know the truth of God.

If you are more fascinated about miracles, you are in danger and I say that despite the fact that I'm a miracle believing preacher with signs and wonders.

It is the knowledge of the Lord that matters but many are just carried away. Jesus said he will say to many, depart from me, I never knew you. The emphasis is on knowing God not just to experience God's miracle.

If all the advert a church has is that they are committed to healing the crippled, such a church lacks glory. If any church has any boast, it should be that they know God. If any man glories, let him glory that he knows me…

The ultimate glory is that he is known.

OUR PRIORITY SHOULD BE MAKING GOD KNOWN

The emphasis of our Christian life should be knowing God.

Only the principles of God and his ways make you know him. Many are just after the abracadabra and the magic.

Jesus said in the last days many will follow miracles. Jesus here was challenging Philip and was working on him. He said look, you are not my disciple if all you are following after is miracles. If you do not want to see the father, then you cannot follow me.

You must follow me because you want to see the father. Every word that Jesus spoke had only one reason and that was to know the father. The words and activities of your church is what we must question, is it still about the father? We should stop promoting miracles like advertisements, how they happened in America, in Japan, in Tokyo and so on and how many people have been healed. If those are the words coming from your leader, then they are misleading you. We should promote and propagate God rather than men.

Many African preachers are guilty of this. Before you follow anybody, find out what they have achieved in the world before they became a miracle working preacher. Find out who they were and the quality of what they have achieved. If you follow people who could not find themselves a job or who were not good at anything and resorted to miracle working job and flaunting themselves, please run away from such.

Would you rather follow the ways of God or the works of God? People who follow the works of God perish in the wilderness. Even if the man of God is genuine like Moses, he may still perish. He was only leading them by miracles. Many people are leading the people just by the works of

God and constantly only parade such before the people. Jesus was working miracles but he pointed the attention of the people to getting to know the father.

Many church leaders want the people to depend on them. They love the people to flock to them for prayers rather than to learn how to pray for themselves.

When you have been going to church for years and you still do not have a personal relationship with God it means you have given birth to the monster called religion. When you have sowed seeds, paid tithes, gone to Prayer Mountains and run after miracles yet you do not know God, it means you have given birth to the monster called religion.

If all your activities are about what you could get for yourself and it is not about converting or how you can benefit humanity, then you have been engaged in religion.

If you truly know God and you have a personal relationship with God, you will convert that relationship into added value to yourself. If you really know God, people will see the product of that knowledge of God.

A GENUINE RELATIONSHIP BEARS FRUITS

If you truly know God, we will see the fruits.

If you are married, the proof that everything is okay is that you have children. It's the same thing, if you have relationship with God that should produce some fruits. The disciples who knew God turned their world around. The fruits of anyone who knows God speaks for them. There is no way you will know God and you will not be changing your country. If truly you know God, You will be transforming the economy, politics and media — the nation will feel your presence and impact.

If you really know God, you will obey God and that changes everything around you.

This lesson was also communicated in one of the parables of Jesus. In Luke 13:6-9

He was looking for conversion, if you have relationship with God it should be converted into fruits, products and results.

In three years, he was specific! If you are not converting those three years into added value, then question your selfishness. What have you produced for God in three years?

Our Christianity must be converted into some fruits, which is when we will not just be religious. Our anointing must be converted into some added value. You must yield some results. Where are the real life results of your Christian experiences? If you do not have real life results, how can we be sure you are a Christian?

These are strong things to consider for your life. Think on this things now so that you will not live a life of regret.

GOLDEN NUGGETS
FROM CHAPTER 7

- Religion is Christianity when it stops converting

- You must work to convert what you know about God and it is through works that your faith can be converted.

- Religion kills because it has no life in it.

- Whenever you stop converting your religious experiences, you give birth to the monster of religion.

- The church may make you a Pastor, but it cannot force you to know God.

- It is possible to pray and not see God and one of the purposes of our prayers is to see God.

- We should promote and propagate God rather than men.

CHAPTER 8

HOW TO FULFILL GOD'S MANDATE ON YOUR LIFE

Inspiration is one thing and you can't control it, but hard work is what keeps the ship moving. Good luck means, work hard.
KEVIN EUBANKS

Many go through life without discovering the mandate of God for their lives. Many die without making any attempt at what God sent them to the earth to do.

How do you discover God's mandate for you and how do you get to fulfill that which God has sent you to do on the earth? That will be the subject of our discussions in this chapter.

It is only through works that a man can fulfill God's mandate upon the earth. There is no substitute for work. If you are going to fulfil God's mandate for you, you need work. If you will accomplish why he sent you to the earth, you only have one instrument. That instrument through which we can fulfill God's mandate and the only instrument through which we can fulfill God's calling on us is work. You must work and you must work very hard to fulfill your purpose.

You must work if you do not want to become a spectator on the earth. You must work if you do not want your life to be a spectating life. Spectators are those who clap for others, they go to stadiums not to be the hero but to clap for those who are actually working. Such people have no time to create their own service or make products which others can applaud. The only thing they want to do is seek someone who is doing something. They kill time and clap for other people who are actually busy. That is unfortunately the life many people are living.

Did you see the new telephone? Have you heard about the latest iPad? Did you see the latest car? Have you seen the newest brand? This is all some people engage in throughout their life.

ACTOR OR SPECTATOR?

Now the question is, are you a spectator or are you an actor in this drama of life? In this drama of life, everyone is supposed to be an actor and in a way supposed to act life out. Those who watch are not adding any value to themselves because spectators only clap. Spectators are not the actors of life, they only look on and applaud or criticize what others do.

Every one of us has been called to be an actor in the drama of life and everyone has a role to play as well. In your own place, you are supposed to be active. The difference between the actor and spectator is that even though both are busy, one is only applauding for the one that is working. Footballers and soccer players make millions of dollars while millions of people look on, cheering the players but still earn nothing. Millions of fans are over themselves, spending a lot to spectate while the people they cheer get wealthier each day.

Only actors are paid. Spectators are not paid.

Spectators loose in the long run. It is one thing for you not to get paid for going to the stadium, but you still lose in the process of spectating. This explains that in life, there is no static point, you are either winning or losing.

This would not have been so funny except for the fact that it is what we see happening in the world today. Many of us live our lives just spectating. Even if you do not go to the soccer stadiums to watch, what about the stadium of life? In the stadium of life, there are only about 3% of humanity who are players. A maximum of 5% of all people are the ones who cause things to happen, they are the movers and shakers. They are those who the world celebrate while the other 95% of people are the ones who go there fighting to be cheerleaders.

Apart from cheering for the actors, they act like people in the physical stadiums by not playing and losing out. In real life, the spectators lose not just their time, they lose their time and life.

Again, no spectator is paid. Many go out to lend their life out for salary, and spend their salary which is a fraction of their life by paying the money back to the actors.

The actors of life are the people who own the supermarkets, the malls, the stalls where spectators come to purchase. They have made deposit points all over the city for the spectators to go drop their pennies. They make available airlines, gas stations, railway stations etcetera. The people who employ you are the same people who have built outlets where they take back everything they pay you for the work you do.

When you are paid 2000 dollars, they have already figured out how to get more than that amount from you before the end of the month. They have built systems called malls, stalls, etcetera to get their money back. This is a way many spectate in life.

The actors engage in aggressive advertisements that push you to think you cannot survive without the things they are offering you. You work very hard for some increase, and eventually when you get a little increase, you start rejoicing, not knowing that the increase they give you will still go back to them.

You end up buying so much, you even put yourself in debt and work overtime or end up borrowing from them.

That marks the very difference between actors and spectators.

BREAKING THE PATTERN

How do you get out of the vicious cycle? You must first make your mind up not to be a spectator.

You must also understand that work is not created for salary, work is not created for job. Work is not created for money neither is it created to get you busy. Work was created in the garden of Eden before compensation of salary and before sin came into existence. Work came as an instrument for fulfilling destiny and accomplishing God's mandate upon your life. Work is the instrument of conversion. Without work, conversion is impossible.

When God made the concept of work in the garden for Adam and Eve, it was made for them to accomplish God's mandate and plans for their lives. God puts within you some abilities and when you were born on the earth, he ensured you were born in a certain environment to equip you for the mandate you were born for. You went to school, you got education, you had development and your parents did their best for you. All these was not just for you get a job and make a living.

There is a reason God put all these investments, abilities, passion and life within you and also put the resources of the earth under you. This is the same reason God sent his son to die for you, he was packaging you for his own purpose and agenda on the earth.

There is no human being sent to the earth just to work for another human. The first assignment for a man on the earth is to discover and get himself equipped for whatever calling and mandate that he carries. You need to discover your mandate, destiny and calling and once it is discovered, it becomes your sphere of influence. It becomes your territory and where you are supposed to cultivate and bring the presence of God into.

There is a purpose for your creation and there is a reason God has put his presence within you. That purpose is to fulfill God's mandate for your life. God said to Jeremiah; before you were put in your mother's womb I had selected you, I ordained you before you were born. Your ordination took place before you were born on the earth.

Women, you need to understand that you do not need a man to marry you before you begin actualizing destiny. You must begin now to actualize the purpose and reason for your birth.

When you discover who you are, you do not need man's ordination or approval, you only need to believe God and step out.

In any sphere of life, though you may seek out a mentor, his input is additional. The reason God invented work is for us to use the creativity, gift and grace of work to cultivate our gifting to manifest and also release the grace of God in the area he has gifted and placed us.

EVERY MAN HAS AN ASSIGNMENT

There is an assignment upon every one of us on the earth. To fulfill our assignment we need the gift of work and work is not just for getting a salary to survive. The gift of work that God has given us is to be used in fulfilling his mandate in our land of promise. Using the gift God gave you to fulfill your calling means you are actualizing your destiny and fulfilling the divine order. Every one of us has a mandate so no one was sent here empty handed. Everyone was sent here with an assignment, even if you were sent to be a cook, a cleaner, a janitor. Every calling on earth is an assignment. It does not matter what you were called to do, the most important thing is to prove your faithfulness to the master. Though temporarily you have a job to learn faithfulness, by working for others or for survival, you should go with the mindset of training. It's important to go with the mindset of acquiring skills to help deal with the promise land you have been given.

Do not believe anyone who says to you that you do not have a calling. That's a lie, you have a calling which was assigned to you before you were born. It is control that makes a man say your calling is only to become a part of his calling. This is why they teach you all sorts of things that will make you become subjective, they put fear in you and manipulate you.

This is why they say you can't have your own vision, and make you sit all week listening to a hero and end up wasted. They are like slave owners, you are not allowed to go anywhere or do whatever God has called you to do. When you try to rise to do what God has called you to do, they fight you.

The most important thing is for you to fulfill your mandate, and the only path is through hard work. Through hard work you discover the essence of God's creation.

THERE IS NO SHORT CUT TO BEING ANOINTED

People lie to you when they say it is anointing you need to actualize your calling. Though you need anointing, without hard work anointing becomes futile. Anointing will not put food on your table neither will it take you places. It is when you work hard that anointing works.

Also, it is a lie when you are told that a man will bless you and cause your calling to be actualized. It does not matter who blesses, affirms or anoints you, if you will not work hard, you will be a nonentity and a mediocre in life. Your only testimony will be of the one or two dollar someone blesses you with. You will not be ruling the earth and you will not be in charge for God. Why should you look forward to the bread and butter someone gives you when you can own the bakery? Your testimony should be that your land is being cultivated. You should be rejoicing at the fact that you are subduing your own land of promise, instead you are reduced to making a living and waiting on men's favor. That is an embarrassment and a shame.

Now, let me talk about this from the scriptures.

Let us see how people we admire fulfilled their own destinies, let us see how they fulfilled their own mandate.

Let us consider Joseph, You think Joseph fulfilled mandate because God loved him? No! He was sold as a slave into Egypt, into the house of Potiphar where he worked as a slave. He worked so hard till he became the best in the place where he was sold into. Even though that was not his calling yet, he was working his way into his calling and destiny.

When he was sent into prison, hard work saw him through his stay there. That is a confirmation that it is only through hard work that we can fulfill God's mandate upon our lives. Even in slavery hard work vindicated Joseph. It vindicated him during betrayal and when he was forgotten also. He kept working very hard. He was so close to God that God revealed Pharaoh's dreams to him though there were other people there as well. Though there were wizards, witches and magicians, they could not give the interpretation of Pharaoh's dreams. Joseph could interpret because he was a friend of God. Joseph was close to God so he could come forward with information. That also is a form of hard work.

There are three forms of work

1. **Spiritual**
2. **Physical**
3. **Mental**

It is obvious that he did his spiritual work well.

When Joseph was in the house of Potiphar, he worked physically. In prison he worked spiritually, and when he was released from the prison, he kept working mentally. Those are the three areas of work where Joseph excelled.

He was able to do all forms of work excellently.

THE POWER OF MENTAL WORK

We can all tell the story of Joseph, and what is often emphasized is how God spoke through him and how he built storage that lasted through 7 years of famine. We almost never talk about the amount of work that goes into that. When Joseph got the revelation of the storage that was supposed to be built, Egypt didn't know how to build it. Even the king had to task Joseph to do it because God had shown him the plan of what was to happen in Egypt. He had discovered the technology that could refrigerate food for the world for 14 years.

The whole world was able to go into Egypt and they were adequately supplied with food through a superb technological concept generated by Joseph's mind. In fact, it is possible that the Pyramids and many other things still in Egypt might have been products of Joseph's hard work. He gave the landmark technology, the systems that could store up all the products that were needed in the time of famine. That is a big technological feat. Can you imagine the amount of math, knowledge of density, gravity and all kinds of scientific laws that must have been considered for enough food to be stored up for the whole earth to be fed? In other words, through hard work Joseph preserved food for the entire earth for 14 solid years. He solved the problem of famine of his day for the entire world. Oh, that we will have such men again.

The foods were not destroyed and didn't get spoilt. He also developed the economics of acquiring the whole land for Pharaoh.

Even now the whole continent of Africa do not have enough food being stored up due to weak refrigeration. In Africa, food is only available in seasons and they are not preserved yet people are in universities and schools. Yet Joseph was self-educated, he worked on the ideas he was given and he built on his revelation.

It doesn't matter the revelation you receive, you still have to work on the process of construction. Anyone can talk about Joseph's revelation, but the revelation was just God's aspect. God gives the revelation but many times the human aspect is neglected. Despite the spectacular revelation, he had to calculate and develop his mind architecturally and mathematically.

Do you know how much of calculation is done by architects and structural engineers in building edifices? How about a storage system for 14 years and the foods were not rotten? Think about such a mind and the depth of mathematics and even in this computer age we still do not know Joseph's pyramids and storage systems. I believe this whole idea originated from Joseph's minds. That is what this whole work is about.

We need to develop our minds with intellectual work to be able to fulfill the mandate of God. I believe if not for the work Joseph did on himself he would not have achieved his mandate. He achieved God's program through self-development and self-education. He succeeded through getting all the wisdom of Egypt and all the wisdom from God till he had a superior mind and was able to do all he needed to do in Egypt.

DO NOT GIVE ROOM FOR LAZINESS

God is not going to come to do all we are supposed to, believing that is fallacy. Despite God showing up, Joseph had to go to work. Despite God showing up, you need to get yourself educated. You need to become the best and go about creating products, and working on adding value to some goods and services. Despite receiving inspiration from God, you need to work out its conversion.

Instead of sitting in those prayer meetings and churches, go to work. It is about hard work. It is only through hard work you can fulfill your destiny. Do not allow anyone waste your life in so called 'miracle services', 'deliverance services', 'midweek services' and all the funny services with funny names. Go to work.

Daniel worked hard. It is only through such work he could achieve all he did in Babylon. He disciplined himself to work hard, he renounced pleasure for a cause and was busy working in the university. He got the knowledge of Egypt and Babylon. To be the best in a foreign country, you've got to work really hard. He got all the wisdom of Babylon, he mastered it so well and he took what he got and added it up to the wisdom he got from the God of Israel.

The wisdom he got from the God of Israel was used with the earthly knowledge from Babylonian universities and he was able to rise up in the land where he was. He fulfilled the mandate and became a ruler in a foreign land.

Let us consider Moses, there is no human seen in the bible who did not work hard to fulfill destiny because there is no bypassing hard work. It is only through hard work we can fulfill the destiny and path God has laid before us. You've got to work hard in the three areas.

Moses was raised in Luxury, but then he left the palace and went on exile. He worked for another man for forty years, tending his sheep. He went through that because he needed the experience to shepherd the children of Israel in the wilderness. He needed the experience to build the first temple in the wilderness. Can you imagine what forty years of work meant? Yet he was faithful and kept working very hard to fulfill all that God wanted him to fulfill.

Look at Solomon, he was a workaholic. Consider David and all the heroes. They all worked very hard.

DO NOT WASTE THE GRACE OF GOD

One very familiar case is that of Apostle Paul, look at what he said in 1 Corinthians 15:10,

"But God was kind! He made me what I am, and his wonderful kindness wasn't wasted. I worked much harder than any of the other apostles, although it was really God's kindness at work and not me." (KJV uses grace)

Hard work is a blessing and a tool to fulfill our mandate. In that scripture, Paul confirmed that work is not a curse but God's blessing on earth.

No man can really work and enjoy the benefit of his land unless he is working 14-16 hours every day. I'm not talking about job, I'm talking about working on your destiny and mission on earth.

Paul said, by grace he is who he is and that grace has enabled him to work that is why it was not in vain. Let me tell you something about grace, everyone has been given grace. He ascended and gave gifts to men. There is no way you will be sent to earth except with some grace to do and accomplish what you have been called to. It does not matter how unbelievable the task is, you have grace to do all that you were born to do.

As a Christian, you have access to greater grace and you can access such grace through right attitude. However grace alone will not do the job. You cannot fulfill your mandate by grace alone. Though Paul said he is who he is by grace, yet he said beyond that it was not in vain. Why did he say that? He was talking about the possibility of wasting the grace of God. That is what some people are doing right now. Some people are reading this book and are wasting the grace of God on their lives?

Some receive grace and are just waiting. Some claim to be waiting for confirmation, a prophetic word! What a misguided thought. They want a supernatural occurrence to happen, maybe somebody will show up with some messages for them. Those are the people that are wasting the grace of God.

What are the things we should be careful of so the grace of God isn't wasted? How do we respond to the grace of God?

Paul also gave the answer.

Paul said *'by grace...'*

Why is the grace of God not in vain? Because I labored. Remember the word *"Labor."*

WORK IS NOT A CURSE

If you say hard work is a curse, are you saying Paul was under a curse?

Why didn't Paul just say one day of favor or grace is better than a thousand years of labor or hard work. Why? Do you think Paul lacked favor or do you think he couldn't claim grace and promises? He had all that, yet despite all that it was his own responsibility to make sure the grace does not become wasted. For the grace not to become squandered and wasted, he needed to work hard. It is the hard work that justifies the grace. The hard work brings about the fulfillment that he labored for more abundantly than the rest of the apostles.

'A day of favor is better than a thousand years of labor' gospel has wasted so many Christians in this generation.

Paul was so serious about labor he knew that grace was not enough, laying hands was not enough, being with Jesus was not enough. Though he was not with Jesus physically like the rest, yet he became the first and overtook the rest of the apostles by the instrumentality of work. What made him become first was hard work. He overtook all those who were into ministry years before him by the tool of work. Being and living with Jesus physically for three and half years did not help them. Even if the trinity were to be living in your room. If your first name were to be Gabriel and you had angels coming to your room, If you do not work hard, nothing works. If you fail to work nothing works.

HARD WORK ACTIVATES GRACE

He said it is the hard work that activated the grace of God upon his own life. He said if you don't work hard the grace will only become latent without any meaningful contribution. The grace will not benefit you anything. It is like talent, your talent will never be enough unless you add work. The guy without talent but strong work ethic will always beat the guy with talent alone.

He said he labored more abundantly than the rest of people. Can you say you are laboring harder than anyone else in your field and area of influence? Can you boldly say you are working more seriously than anyone else who is competing with you?

Some charismatics say unbelievers work hard because there is no grace, what about Paul? He had grace like we have, yet that was no excuse not to work very hard. It does not matter the amount of anointing, it will be latent. Nothing will happen and there will be no result or reward if the anointing lacks work.

Jesus said I must work the works of him that sent me .... My Father worketh hitherto, and I work.

It is the instrumentality God has given to us. No going around it, no short cuts, no laying of hands, no amount of service, no amount of prophecy, without hard work everything else goes to waste.

If you do not work hard, nothing works.

This principle made Paul become the best among the rest. The grace was upon him to work. Grace is released more abundantly as you work. For more grace to be released, you've got to work harder.

It is only through hard work that we fulfill destiny and mandate.

That is the formula of God.

Even in the Garden of Eden, Adam and Eve had to work hard to fulfill their destiny and up till today there is no exception.

My dear reader, now you see that it very possible to be an inventor and a co-creator with God. It is possible to convert all of your internal energies into products. It is possible to daily rain down products upon this earth. It is possible to unleash all of your potential and to release all that you carry within you.

Please do not forget this, if there is one thing that you must always remember now that you have read this book, it is the power and the essence of hard work. It is real hard work that will release your potential.

I don't count my sit-ups; I only start counting when it starts hurting because they're the only ones that count. That is how to become a champion.
MUHAMMAD ALI

Hard work is one of the greatest principles which I have carefully guided my life by. I have discovered that life will be a total waste without working very hard. I realize that everything good in me will be dead without hard work. I also realize that hard work is the only way I can express all that I carry within me. Now, I have got so much reservoir of treasure within me that I wonder if just a lifetime will be enough to exhaust them. Hence, I work extremely hard every day to express all the virtues that I carry within me. At the end of each day, I want to have done in that day what many people cannot do in a lifetime.

Success is built on hard work, the right hard work itself is success. Hard work is the secret of being a genius. Thomas Edison said that being a genius is ten percent inspiration and ninety percent perspiration and hard work. That is a principle right there and no one on earth can beat it.

This is same secret of the men we have considered so far in this book, Bill Gates and Steve Jobs.

It has been said over and again that Bill Gates worked a minimum of sixteen hours every day while building Microsoft and this work ethic which began at a very early age continued till he was into his thirties. In fact, according to him, he never took a day off from his work till he was more than thirty.

I read a story a long time ago about a new employee coming to work at his company, Microsoft and complaining that there was somebody who stays back in the office, working and sleeping under his office desk. Supposedly it was Bill Gates. Bill Gates often worked many times over the night under his work desk while all his employees went home. He worked at weekends too. He often would boast that he never stayed away from the office for up to 7 hours any day.

That is how you become an inventor and a creator. If you want to become a Bill Gates, start working productively at least sixteen hours every day.

It was same secret that produced Steve Jobs. Steve Jobs had an incredible work ethic. He worked from 7 a.m. to 9 p.m. every day. Steve Jobs never thought of work as a job. He thought of it more as his religion and his hobby. His passion for work made him a workaholic, he took no time off and would never pick phone calls in the middle of the night.

He demanded perfection in little things and that was how he worked. He not only worked hard, but he worked relentlessly. Fearless and focused, he was ready to fire any employee just to get the job done. Many people quit working for him because he was so intense.

Now you see that success is not accidental. Success is not magic either.

*The heights that great men reached and
kept were not attained in sudden flight but,
they while their companions slept, they
were toiling upwards in the night.*
HENRY WADSWORTH LONGFELLOW

It is my hope that this examples and illustrations will change the course of your life forever. You cannot afford to die without being an inventor. If you will not waste the whole of your life and existence, then you must quickly and urgently become a workaholic like Bill Gates and Steve Jobs.

I anticipate all that you will become just because you have read this book. I anticipate all the inventions that will come through you in your lifetime. I anticipate that you will live your life differently and that the world will never be the same again just because of your existence. I anticipate that you too will change the world just like Bill Gates and Steve Jobs have done. I anticipate that you will be in the next generation of men like Bill Gates and Steve Jobs. Arise now, go show the world what you carry and what you can do. I am excited for you already. Blessings.

GOLDEN NUGGETS
FROM CHAPTER 8

- Many die without making any attempt at what God sent them to the earth to do.

- Every one of us has been called to be an actor in the drama of life and everyone has a role to play as well.

- There is a reason God put all these investments, abilities, passion and life within you and also put the resources of the earth under you.

- There is no human being sent to the earth just to work for another human.

- Do not believe anyone who says to you that you do not have a calling.

- No man can really work and enjoy the benefit of his land unless he is working 14-16 hours every day.

- If you fail to work nothing works.

INFORMATION ABOUT THE EMBASSY OF GOD CHURCH AND PASTOR SUNDAY ADELAJA

Pastor Sunday Adelaja — The only black man in the world that leads a congregation of mostly Caucasians in 50 countries. Below are some facts about Pastor Sunday's life and ministry.

- Pastor Sunday is the pastor of the largest Evangelical Church in Europe with a population of 99.9% white Europeans in Kiev Ukraine.
- His ministry has charity units that feed over 5000 people on a daily basis.
- Through his ministry over 30 thousand people have been delivered from drug and alcohol addictions.
- He helped raise over 200 millionaires in US dollars in his church, most of whom were former drug/ alcohol addicts and societal outcasts.
- He has raised a global movement that is influencing over 70 million people around the globe.
- Branches of his church are in over 50 countries.
- He has spoken in different nations of the world on National Transformation.
- Pastor Sunday is one of the few, if not the only African, who has ever spoken in the US senate.
- Pastor Sunday is one of the few African pastors who has spoken on the floor of the UN.
- He has addressed the Japanese Members of parliament.
- He has spoken in the Knesset to members of Israeli parliament. The list goes on and on.
- His ministry has over 500 hundred government officials holding different government positions in Ukraine.
- He has written and published over 300 books and recorded thousands of messages.

THE EMBASSY OF GOD CHURCH

There are more than 300 rehabilitation centers for alcohol and drug addicts which have been operational in Ukraine and Europe since 1994.

More than 20 000 people recovered from their addictions, and became normal members of the society. Thanks to the rehabilitation centers opened by the church.

There are homes for abandoned street children operated by the church which have successfully reunited more than 5 000 children with their families.

The Embassy of God Church is involved in many social projects that are directed at maintaining family values, active civil involvement and individual fulfillment of church members.

Many former members of mafia organizations and criminals have become devout Christians through the missionary work of the Embassy of God Church.

The church's hot-line has counseled over a 200,000 people.

Right now there are over 25,000 members in the Embassy of God Church Kyiv, Ukraine.

BIOGRAPHY OF PASTOR SUNDAY ADELAJA

Pastor Sunday Adelaja is the Founder and Senior Pastor of The Embassy of the Blessed Kingdom of God for All Nations Church in Kyiv, Ukraine.

He is a Nigerian-born leader with an apostolic gift for the twenty-first century. In his mid thirties Pastor Sunday had already proven to be one of the world's most dynamic communicators and church planters and is regarded as the most successful pastor in Europe with over 25,000 members as well as daughter and satellite churches in over 50 countries worldwide.

The congregation includes members from all spheres of society, from former drug and alcohol addicts, to politicians and millionaires. It's high percentage of white Europeans (99%), also indicates that boundaries of racial prejudice have been surpassed. In the same country where Pastor Sunday was called "chocolate rabbit" and several attempts have been made to deport him, thousands join hands and support his mission to see Ukraine and the whole world affected and saved by the gospel of the Kingdom. Pastor Sunday is recognized as an unusually gifted teacher of the Word of God, with an extraordinary operation in the gifts of the Spirit, especially the word of knowledge. He receives numerous speaking invitations to several countries in all continents of the world yearly, as well as invitations to meetings with heads of States and other Politicians.

Pastor Sunday's influence in the areas of church growth, prayer and evangelism has been noted by Charisma Magazine, Ministries Today and many other Christian periodicals. The secular world media, such as the Wall Street Journal, Forbes, Washington Post, Reuters, Associated Press, CNN, BBC and German, Dutch and French national television have all widely reported on him. The Wall Street Journal called him *"A Man with a Mission"* set out to save Kyiv. The Ukrainian President Yushenko acknowledged his strong involvement in the Orange revolution for democracy in Ukraine. Former Mayor of New York City Rudolph Giuliani stated: *"Sunday, God bless you in your important mission. When I next come to Ukraine I would like to be at your church"*.

In August 2007 by invitation from the employees of the UN, Pastor Sunday Adelaja was invited as a speaker for three sessions. It was the first time in the history of the UN that a pastor speaks in the main hall of the UN. There were 500 organizations and missions from different parts of the world and leaders from 30 countries that participated in these sessions. From then on, the Embassy of God started its preparation to enter the UN and become a member of this organization.

Pastor Sunday's passion for National Transformation has driven him to maximally spread the word of God. He has written and published over 200 books of which some have been translated to English, German, Chinese, Arabic and Dutch. Also, thousands of sermons have been recorded. He organizes annual pastors leadership seminars where over 1,000 ministers regularly attend, studying the topic 'Pastoring without Tears'. His passion is to ignite these ministers with fire and power to transform their cities and countries.

Every year Pastor Sunday organizes Pastor's Seminars that take place in the church. He is also the main speaker there. During this time more than 1 000 Ministers learn how to be a pastor without tears, and learn the keys of achieving success. Also, every year Pastor Sunday organizes a summer and winter fast which aims at equipping Ministers with fire and power to change their cities and countries.

Nowadays, the apostolic ministry of Pastor Sunday has gone far beyond the boundaries of Ukraine, making him a desirable speaker and a Pastor to Pastors in many nations of the world. To date, he has visited over 50 countries.

Pastor Sunday is happily married to his "Princess" Abosede, and they are blessed with three children: Perez, Zoe and Pearl.

Below is the link to a photo gallery of Pastor Sunday and other likeminded individuals who have also positively impacted their nations:

http://www.godembassy.com/media/photo/view-album/3.html

Bill Clinton —
42Nd President Of The
United States (1993–2001),
Former Arcansas State
Governor

Ariel "Arik" Sharon —
Israeli Politician, Israeli
Prime Minister (2001–2006)

Benjamin Netanyahu —
Statesman Of Israel. Israeli
Prime Minister (1996–1999),
Acting Prime Minister
(From 2009)

Jean ChrEtien —
Canadian Politician,
20^Th Prime Minister Of
Canada, Minister Of Justice
Of Canada, Head Of Liberan
Party Of Canada

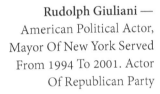

Rudolph Giuliani —
American Political Actor,
Mayor Of New York Served
From 1994 To 2001. Actor
Of Republican Party

Colin Powell —
Is An American Statesman
And A Retired Four-Star
General In The Us Army,
65^Th United States Secretary
Of State

Peter J. Daniels — Is A Well-Known And Respected Australian Christian International Business Statesman Of Substance

Madeleine Korbel Albright — An American Politician And Diplomat, 64ᵀʰ United States Secretary Of State

Kenneth Robert Livingstone — An English Politician, 1ˢᵗ Mayor Of London (4 May 2000 – 4 May 2008), Labour Party Representative

Sir Richard Charles Nicholas Branson —
English Business Magnate, Investor And Philanthropist. He Founded The *Virgin Group,* Which Controls More Than 400 Companies

Mel Gibson —
American Actor And Filmmaker

Chuck Norris —
American Martial Artist, Actor, Film Producer And Screenwriter

Christopher Tucker —
American Actor
And Comedian

Bernice Albertine King —
American Minister Best
Known As The Youngest
Child Of Civil Rights Leaders
Martin Luther King Jr. And
Coretta Scott King Andrew

Andrew Young — American
Politician, Diplomat, And
Activist, 14[Th] United States
Ambassador To The United
Nations, 55[Th] Mayor Of
Atlanta

General Wesley Kanne Clark — 4-Star General And Nato Supreme Allied Commander

FOLLOW
SUNDAY ADELAJA
ON SOCIAL MEDIA

Subscribe And Read Pastor Sunday's Blog:
www.sundayadelajablog.com

**Follow these links and listen to over 200
of Pastor Sunday's Messages free of charge:**
http://sundayadelajablog.com/content/

Follow Pastor Sunday on Twitter:
www.twitter.com/official_pastor

Join Pastor Sunday's Facebook page to stay in touch:
www.facebook.com/pastor.sunday.adelaja

**Visit our websites for more information
about Pastor Sunday's ministry:**
http://www.godembassy.com
http://www.pastorsunday.com
http://sundayadelaja.de

CONTACT

FOR DISTRIBUTION OR TO ORDER
BULK COPIES OF THIS BOOK,
PLEASE CONTACT US:

USA
CORNERSTONE PUBLISHING
info@thecornerstonepublishers.com
+1 (516) 547-4999
www.thecornerstonepublishers.com

AFRICA
Sunday Adelaja Media Ltd.
E-mail: btawolana@hotmail.com
+2348187518530, +2348097721451, +2348034093699

LONDON, UK
Pastor Abraham Great
abrahamagreat@gmail.com
+447711399828, +441908538141

KIEV, UKRAINE
pa@godembassy.org
Mobile: +380674401958

Best Selling Books by Dr. Sunday Adelaja
Available on Amazon.com and Okadabooks.com

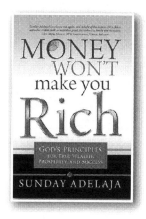

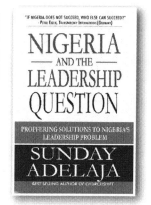

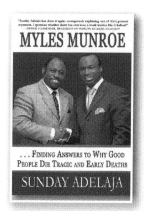

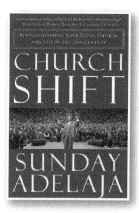

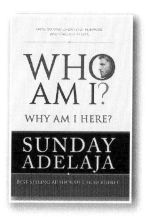

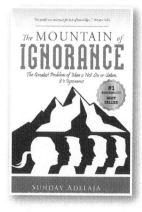

Best Selling Books by Dr. Sunday Adelaja
Available on Amazon.com and Okadabooks.com

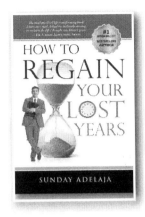

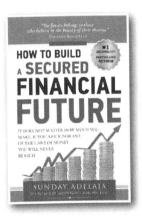

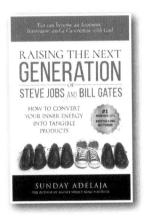

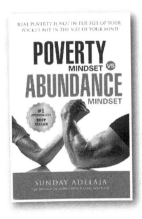

Made in the USA
San Bernardino, CA
03 July 2017